Creating Community

The Bible Reading Fellowship
15 The Chambers, Vineyard
Abingdon OX14 3FE
brf.org.uk

The Bible Reading Fellowship (BRF) is a Registered Charity (233280)

ISBN 978 0 85746 009 7
First published 2013
Reprinted 2014, 2017, 2018
10 9 8 7 6 5 4 3
All rights reserved

Acknowledgements
Unless otherwise stated, scripture quotations are from The New Revised Standard
Version of the Bible, Anglicised edition, copyright © 1989, 1995 by the Division of
Christian Education of the National Council of the Churches of Christ in the United
States of America. Used by permission. All rights reserved.

Scripture quotations are taken from The Holy Bible, New International Version
(Anglicised edition) copyright © 1979, 1984, 2011 by Biblica. Used by permission of
Hodder & Stoughton Publishers, a Hachette UK company. All rights reserved. 'NIV' is
a registered trademark of Biblica. UK trademark number 1448790.

Extracts from the Authorised Version of the Bible (The King James Bible), the rights
in which are vested in the Crown, are reproduced by permission of the Crown's
Patentee, Cambridge University Press.

Every effort has been made to trace and contact copyright owners for material used
in this resource. We apologise for any inadvertent omissions or errors, and would
ask those concerned to contact us so that full acknowledgement can be made in
the future.

A catalogue record for this book is available from the British Library

Printed and bound by CPI Group (UK) Ltd, Croydon CR0 4YY

Creating Community

Ancient ways for modern churches

Simon Reed

This book is dedicated to the most important people of all: Alison and Matt, and in memory of Emma. It's also for the people of the Ascension, Hanger Hill, and St Mary's, West Twyford, and for all the members of the Community of Aidan and Hilda: without you, none of this would even have begun. Thanks for sharing the journey.

Contents

Foreword

This book could be entitled *From the Ordinary Church: a Way of Life*. Its author shares the vision that the local church is the hope of the world and that each church can find its distinctive vocation. He observes that whereas many contemporary churches try to attract a crowd and then turn it into a community, the early churches in Celtic lands started as small communities and then gathered wider numbers.

But can our long-established small churches become living communities? From his own experience, Simon argues that they can if they adopt three practices – a Way of Life, a network of Soul Friends and a rhythm of prayer. He establishes that a Way of Life coheres with New Testament practice and explores how to develop it.

I know Simon as a friend and colleague in The Community of Aidan and Hilda, which has Catholic, Orthodox and Evangelical members. He tells his personal story from within his own tradition. Always (and this is so refreshing) he is more concerned with the product than with the label.

The book is timely, for, as the author points out, the moral disintegration that underlies the unravelling of community and society could herald a new dark age. Winston Churchill, when his country had its back to the wall during World War II, famously said 'Give us the tools and we will finish the job.' Simon gives us some tools. Let us, the readers, help to finish the job.

Ray Simpson
Holy Island of Lindisfarne
www.raysimpson.org

Introduction

At 11.30am on 29 May 1953 Edmund Hillary and Tenzing Norgay stood on the summit of Mount Everest, 8848 metres above sea level, the first men to reach the roof of the world. Their names are well known all over the globe but their achievement would have been impossible without another man whose name is known only to other mountaineers. His name was Eric Shipton and without him Everest would not have been climbed for many more years.

Since the 1920s, expeditions had tried to climb the world's highest mountain from the north, approaching from Tibet and trying to ascend its difficult north-east ridge. In 1951, when access through the kingdom of Nepal was finally permitted, Eric Shipton led an expedition to try to find a way up the mountain from the south. With great determination they explored the vast glacial valley known as the Western Cwm and bravely picked their way through the forbidding ice towers and crevasses of the massive glacier known as the Khumbu Icefall. Having got to the end, they didn't go on to climb Everest, but for the first time they saw a route to the summit which looked as if it would work.

Writing this book feels like reporting on that Reconnaissance Expedition. I want to tell you about something I've seen but haven't yet reached. It's the story of a journey in progress whose outcome will not be clear for some years yet, but I hope that it will inspire you to set off in search of a place I think is worth reaching.

I climb mountains for fun – smaller ones than Everest, I must admit – but my day job is rather harder. I'm a church leader and my goal is to help people deepen their connection with God and each other, and connect God with the whole of life. I've tried lots of different ways of doing it but I'm always on the lookout for better tools to use in making disciples and creating community. For more than ten years I've drawn inspiration from Celtic spirituality through my membership of the international Community of Aidan and Hilda and it's from this contemporary expression of Britain's spiritual roots that I've gained the insights I want to share in this book.

There's much talk today of 'new ways of being church'. As I've explored the Celtic roots of the Christian faith in the British Isles in community with others who are inspired by our spiritual ancestors, I've realised that the third-millennium church has much in common with the first-millennium church, and, more importantly, much to learn from it. I want to introduce you to a new but very old way of being church which is based upon a Way of Life, a network of Soul Friends, and a rhythm of prayer. These are the building blocks of what many are now calling a 'new monastic' spirituality. I believe that their rediscovery offers a vital key which opens up an ancient way for modern churches, one which makes grown-up Christians and creates genuine and lasting community.

Chapter 1

Making disciples and building communities

Martin came to an Alpha Course, drawn, I imagine, by its invitation to explore the meaning of life. He was absolutely convinced that he had no need to become a Christian, but after the course he decided he wanted to stay in touch. We would meet for lunch from time to time and Martin would talk about his own journey to find meaning and purpose in life. One of his favourite approaches was to turn the conversation round and ask me for my answers to the probing questions he was asking himself. As a result I found myself one day putting down a steak sandwich to consider what I thought the purpose and focus of my life was. 'What are you here to do?' asked Martin with his usual quizzical smile.

Studying theology does give you a head start in situations like this. The classic statement from the 17th-century Westminster Catechism flickered through my mind: 'Man's chief end is to glorify God, and to enjoy him forever.' That answer was not going to satisfy Martin. I'd need to explain what it meant and he was already sceptical of anything he felt was simply dogma. Only something personal would do. I did a quick rewind, reviewing my life as a Christian, and was faintly surprised by how quickly and how clearly the answer came: 'Helping people connect with God.'

I have never needed convincing about the importance of evangelism because I would not be a Christian without it. I don't mean big tub-thumping rallies full of emotional hype and psychological manipulation – the negative and largely inaccurate image that many people have of evangelism, both in the church and outside. What I mean is the simple process of ordinary Christians sharing their faith, as opportunities arise, with those who don't yet believe, in obedience to Jesus' command to 'go and make disciples of all nations' (Matthew 28:19). That's how I discovered Christian faith as a teenager and so my understanding from the very start has been that if you get connected with God, you want other people to make the same connection and you do whatever you can to help them.

In the years that have followed it's been my privilege to see God at work in a variety of settings, from the hot-house environment of university life to the grim urban depression of 1980s Merseyside and then through the early days of introducing the Alpha course in a Buckinghamshire market town. My relationship with the church has been a surprising journey. Occasional childhood experiences of a village church whose worship was as fossilised as its building was ancient left me with the impression that going to church was as spiritually beneficial as watching paint dry. Thankfully some better experiences elsewhere brought me to a different opinion but it was still something of a jolt when, after two very exciting years as a full-time church and youth worker, God made it unmistakably clear that the next step was to train as an Anglican minister.

Since then, my convictions about the church have come a long way. Bill Hybels, founding pastor of the innovative and influential Willow Creek Community Church in Barrington, Illinois, has famously written that 'the local church is the hope of the world', and I would wholeheartedly subscribe to that view. Christianity is irreducibly something we do together. Our faith in Christ must be personal or it is nothing, but it is lived out and matured in relationship with other people. The word 'you' in the New Testament is nearly always plural, and, whatever some scholars argue, the overwhelming conclusion is that the ministry of Jesus was about calling people *together* to express the life of the coming kingdom of God. So whether it's good, bad or indifferent, we end up with the church, which means not a building – useful as they are – but the *ekklesia* (from which we get our word 'ecclesiastical'), the congregation or gathering together of God's people. God's church is at the heart of God's plan for God's creation, so for me it's a no-brainer that we need to find ways to enable it to reach its full God-intended potential.

For that reason, although my first taste of church leadership was in a relatively large church which was regarded as 'successful' and saw itself as a local flagship of the 1990s renewal movement, I was not looking for more of the same when I moved on. There were still many churches struggling to catch up with a fast-changing world and, if renewal meant anything, it had to mean something in these settings. That was how, in 1996, I ended up with a new job in Ealing, West London, with not one but two churches to look after.

The Church of the Ascension, Hanger Hill, close to West London's most famous Gyratory system, and St Mary's, West Twyford, were both churches whose first instinct was to describe themselves as 'traditional'. St Mary's needed to be. Its structurally flawed building had been closed on safety grounds the previous year and the elderly remnant of the congregation were meeting in a back room of the run-down church hall. The past was all they had to hang on to, but they were very determined not to give up. The Ascension was in better shape but the congregation were aware that they had seen better days. What marked out both of these otherwise unremarkable churches was that they did not want things to stay as they were. Neither had a clear sense of what change would mean, but both understood that it was necessary if they were to reach out to their neighbourhoods and draw new people into the Christian family. What a journey we've been on since! The greatest compliment I can pay to this diverse and endlessly interesting and engaging bunch of people is that they have allowed their churches bit by bit to change, almost beyond recognition from what they were, as together we have gone in search of God's best for us and for the people who don't yet know him.

There's more than one way to grow

When you're a small church it's very easy to feel patronised and demoralised by bigger churches who are able to do all kinds of things that you can't, simply because they have more people and more resources. In recent years various people have written in praise of the small church and told us it's OK to be small. 'A tangerine shouldn't feel bad that it's not an orange.' It's not my place to judge (no, really!), but I did think it was slightly ironic that just after the publication of one such book and the accompanying speaking tour, the author went off to become the minister of a very large church somewhere else! The reality is, however, that if small churches don't add new members to replace those who will inevitably move on, they will decline and die. More than that, according to Jesus we're in the disciple-making business, and it seems obvious to me that if we don't add some new disciples to the process from one year to the next, it's hard to see how we're doing our job.

This was brought into sharp focus at the beginning of the millennium when, in the year 2000, I visited Lindisfarne, England's historic Holy Island, to attend an intriguing conference called 'Celtic Models for Emerging Churches' led by Ray Simpson of the Community of Aidan and Hilda. It was a week full of insight and inspiration but what got my attention in the first session was the conclusion from the most recent national church survey that, in the next few decades, some 20,000 small to medium-sized churches were likely to close. Their only hope was to change. You won't be surprised to know that my priority during some personal free time was to start praying with a fair degree of intensity that we'd be one of those that made it through.

I learned a lot that week about what the first-millennium British church has got to offer the third-millennium British church. The starting point for me was that these early Celtic Christian communities in Ireland, Wales and Scotland were all different, and each had its own sense of calling. We were given the challenge to go back and discern God's distinctive calling for us. Find that and, whatever it was, we'd know we had a future of some sort.

Vision has become a rather jaded term, perhaps because of the way it has found its way into modern management-speak. 'Our vision is to deliver the perfect pork pie' may be a valid commercial goal but it's hardly inspirational. I'm happy to go on using the word but perhaps it's more helpful, and certainly more biblical, to think in terms of *vocation*: what is it that God is calling us to be and to do? If we ask that question of a church, there will always be a great deal of similarity and overlap because there are certain things which all churches are called to do – worship, pray, teach, care for one another, and so on. Yet there will always be the personal nuance, the distinctive call from God. The important thing is to identify and express it in a way which speaks to us.

Vision is rarely received instantly. There are times when God speaks with amazing clarity, but even then you need to spend time thinking through what he has said. As I tried to discern God's vision for our church, I wanted to be sure that every word I wrote truly reflected as far as humanly possible God's distinctive call to us, and that it was genuinely owned by the members of the church. In 2002 'A Vision for the Ascension' was presented to a core group of the congregation, who received it with great positivity. Our headline statement, which was then unpacked in greater detail, was an aspiration to be 'a Christian community committed to praying, welcoming, and growing'. I had no idea at the time just how much meaning was packed into those nine words.

Since then, that core vision has given birth to three successive 'Mission Action Plans' designed to help us progressively to realise more fully each of the three elements of the vision. During that time there have been encouraging signs of God at work. We've seen a greater confidence in prayer and a greater creativity in worship. There has been a slow growth in confidence in inviting others to events like the Alpha course. The age range of the congregation has widened, involving a greater number of children and teenagers but without losing our older members. Most exciting of all has been a project to reorder the church building to create a 'welcome area' at the back with a kitchen and lounge space. I'm excited by this because building projects often start from the minister and have to drag the congregation with them. This project was birthed by members of the church who were thinking through what it meant to be welcoming and decided that the building would have to change. I didn't remotely disagree with them about that, but the important thing was that the idea came from them and was carried through by them, and the motive was to make the church more accessible to those who didn't normally use it.

One of the most important insights I gained through the whole process was that there is a close relationship between growing spiritually and growing in numbers. This might seem an obvious point, but in practice it is often hard to pin down solid evidence of the link. The first two years after we began to implement our vision brought much positive activity and energy but no growth in numbers. At the time, we had a trainee minister on placement with us and she spoke warmly about all she experienced here but expressed her amazement that there weren't more people. I couldn't figure out what was wrong. Shortly afterwards I came across a church survey tool developed in Germany called Natural Church Development.[1] This approach argues, on the basis of extensive international research, that growth in numbers is linked to the quality characteristics of churches, and it offers statistically validated tools for measuring them. The eight significant areas are identified as empowering leadership, gift-orientated ministry, passionate spirituality, functional structures, inspiring worship services, holistic small groups, need-orientated evangelism, and loving relationships. Grow the quality, Christian Schwarz argues, and the numbers will follow.

The results of the survey told us that we were encouragingly strong in a number of areas but that our biggest perceived weakness was in the category of 'passionate spirituality', and this was holding us back. We had many discussions about what precisely the term means – and it has nothing to do with how loud you can shout or how high you can raise your arms (not that there's anything wrong with either!). The bottom line was that many of our people, even those who had been Christians and members of the church for a long time, did not feel a closeness or confidence in their relationship with God. They didn't feel they had a good connection. The extraordinary and wonderful thing was that as soon as we began to address this issue, we began, very modestly, to grow in numbers, and this growth continued for several years. It's been memorably said that 'to reach for God is to reach God'.[2] It seemed that God was honouring our desire to connect more deeply with him in order to connect more effectively with others, even before we had managed to translate it into definite action.

That discovery led me into a fresh understanding of vision generally and of our vision. I realised that vision isn't just about identifying a target and charting a course towards it, but also about seeing what lies beyond it. If our life with God is a journey, then it's helpful not only to find ways of checking our progress but also to think about where we're trying to go. Out of my struggles to participate in the mission of God in our small church, I began to identify common challenges and fresh ideas which resonated with other people as well. As I explored them in conversation with other church leaders, and then at seminars and conferences, I saw these ideas strike a chord.

The two big questions

The first big question which seems to be exercising everyone's mind, both in the church and in wider society, is how we create, maintain and deepen a genuine and lasting community. This seems to be the holy grail for which everyone is searching.

We live in an increasingly individualistic and fragmented culture but there is still a longing for community, even if we're not sure what it is. It's easy to criticise social networking though the internet, but we must not overlook the underlying desire and need to connect with one another, which is as strong as ever. A little while ago I registered some new software and received an email saying 'Welcome to the *Serif* community'. A community made up of people who don't know each other but all use the same publishing software isn't much of a community, but the use of the word tells us that they think people will respond to it in a positive way. When David Cameron became Prime Minister of the United Kingdom on 11 May 2010, he declared, 'I want us to build a society with stronger families and stronger communities' and described 'rebuilding community' as one of his core values. During the election campaign, Gordon Brown, the previous Prime Minister, argued that his party would protect the 'universal services which gives us something beyond price – a sense of community'. The 2011 riots in many British cities threw these issues into an even sharper and more urgent focus. There may be conflicting visions of what exactly community is in the social sense, and even less consensus on how it is to be achieved, but there is agreement that people feel deeply that it is important. At bottom we all have a need to belong and, however privatised our lives become, that need does not go away.

Community is also the holy grail of the church. I once worked with a vicar who said that he used to think of local church ministry as being like having a group of people sitting on a giant mushroom while he rushed around the bottom to stop them sliding off. They needed something to stick them together – and that something is community. It's also a particular challenge for an eclectic church like ours, where an increasing number of the congregation (currently about one-third) live outside the geographical area of our parish, in a part of London where a two-mile journey can take an hour unless you're happy to walk. Getting people together in one place more than once a week is often surprisingly difficult.

The second big question is how we create mature adult disciples of Jesus Christ – people who are deeply connected with God and find ways to connect every area of their lives to God. In Colossians 1:28, Paul writes that 'it is he [Christ] whom we proclaim, warning and teaching everyone in all wisdom, so that we may present everyone mature in Christ'. This is the core pastoral task in Christian ministry and in our present climate we often struggle to do it successfully. We have excellent tools to help people find Christian faith. Alpha, Emmaus and other similar processes have touched the lives of hundreds of thousands of people. The problem is what to do next. We can run a follow-up course but, despite the spread of Alpha, there is no universal agreement on what to use. We can try various kinds of home group structures, but many churches find them hard to sustain over time and, at every stage, people drop out of the process. Research indicates that even in churches with a very strong home group structure, only half the members at best join a group. The cell church idea has tried basing everything around small groups but, unless a church is starting from scratch, it seems to take a huge amount of restructuring to adopt this model.

Looking back, it's frightening to see how many of my friends who were fired-up Christians at the age of 21 had wandered away from Christ by the time they were 30. Add to that the number of older Christians who have been church members for decades and yet have only the vaguest understanding of their faith and how to live it out. Add to that the number of Christians who can quote chunks of the Bible but never get beyond one-line answers to the complex issues we all face in life, and we've got a big problem. In a recent conversation with a senior leader in my own part of the church, she expressed the view that discipleship is the biggest issue in Christian ministry today.

Finding out how to create community and make mature disciples is therefore absolutely essential to the well-being of our churches and to our own well-being as individual followers of Christ.

The one key insight

It's easy to criticise the church growth movement for being obsessed with numbers and techniques, but, as I pointed out previously, if we're not seeing more people becoming followers of Christ, then we're not carrying out the task he gave us to do. Serious study of the factors that influence church growth originated in the United States, and in the 1980s and 1990s a lot of ideas and influences about church growth and wider renewal came from the other side of the Atlantic. There were many useful insights and I would be the first to acknowledge a great debt of gratitude in particular to John Wimber and the Vineyard movement for all that they gave the British church. Particularly associated with the healing ministry and an emphasis on 'signs and wonders', John Wimber's deepest passion was to see people become Christians and devote every part of their life to God in practical action. From his teaching, also, I first learned the principle that the growth of the body of Christ is inseparably linked to the health of the body of Christ.

Nevertheless, as time went on I found myself growing more and more aware that help from across the Atlantic was limited in its effectiveness. In the first place there are immense cultural differences between the USA and the United Kingdom. Some 40 per cent of Americans have some kind of church involvement compared to between five and 15 per cent of people in the UK, depending on which statistics you use. Knowledge of the Bible is also proportionately greater and Christianity is more highly valued in public life. Tony Blair, according to his spokesman Alistair Campbell, famously 'didn't do God' in his public life, whereas an American President gains support if he attends a prayer breakfast and affirms his personal faith. When Rick Warren, author of *The Purpose Driven Church*,[3] a book which thousands of church leaders have read, started Saddleback Valley Community Church in Orange County, California, he researched the local community and sent a mailshot to 15,000 people offering them a church for people who wanted a new style of church. Two hundred people turned up to the first service!

There is a lot of useful insight and wisdom in Rick Warren's book, but there is no way that such an approach would get the same results here. Our culture of churchgoing has eroded far more than theirs. People need much more to get them even interested.

Secondly, a great deal of material from America originates in large churches, and what works in a large church often does not work in a small one. I nearly laughed out loud at one church leadership conference where we were offered a seminar to help us overcome the pitfalls of recruiting Christian 'superstars' on to our church leadership teams. At that time I was the team and our income wasn't even enough to cover the cost of employing me, let alone recruiting anyone else. I felt like I was visiting a very alien planet.

Thirdly, a great many American churches are entirely independent, a product of the entrepreneurial and pioneering spirit which is so much a part of their culture. Many British churches are part of long-established denominations with particular structures and practices, and individual congregations may well have existed for over a hundred years with all of their accumulated history and tradition. Quite simply we often do not have the freedom to start from scratch in the way that many American churches and movements have been able to do.

This is not meant as an attack on American Christianity, which has many real strengths and can still offer us fresh perspectives. It is merely an observation that there are serious limitations on the help it can give to those outside its national borders. I have a further frustration with the church growth movement in general, despite all the good it has done in offering insights and calling us back to our core task. It is simply that all too often the message coming from 'successful' churches, wherever they are in the world, is 'Become like us and you will definitely grow too.' I heard the pastor of a church numbering many thousands, from a city in the American Midwest, tell a British audience that if he were to take over the leadership of any of our churches for one year, it would be absolutely certain to increase in numbers. Perhaps the politest thing I can say about that is that I'd love to see him try, and I doubt if he ever has done or genuinely intends to do so. Churches, like individual Christians, are amazingly diverse, and one size can never fit all. So how on earth do we realise the potential of all, and how do we join these multi-faceted bricks into a stable building?

As I reflected on this question, it dawned on me that the answer lay not across the seas but across the centuries. I realised that I already knew something growing in our own soil which was creating real community and nurturing genuine and incredibly diverse spiritual growth.

For the past ten years I have been a member of the international Community of Aidan and Hilda, a dispersed and cross-denominational network of Christians who draw inspiration from the Celtic expression of Christianity which flourished in the British Isles in the first millennium. CA&H isn't a church but, as I thought about it, I realised that what I had learned and experienced as a member of this community seemed to hold the key to unlocking answers to our two big questions – creating genuine and lasting community, and making mature disciples of Jesus. Drawing on the ancient wisdom of the Celtic Christians and recasting it for the 21st century, I began to see practical ways of achieving these two vital goals.

An ancient and new way of being church

The Community of Aidan and Hilda emerged in the early 1990s, as a network of people already involved in various creative ways in the renewal of the church found fresh inspiration in the early church of the British Isles. Celtic Christianity has become very well known in the years since then and much has been written about it, some of it quite naive and romantic, and some of it a highly critical reaction to that naivety. Two well-written and accessible introductions are *The Celtic Way* by respected church historian Ian Bradley and *Exploring*

Celtic Spirituality by Ray Simpson, the founding Guardian of the Community of Aidan and Hilda.[4] Both attempt to be accurate about what these inspiring early Christians were really like, but also to apply what they can teach us to today.

Many things drew me to this community. One feature of the church in Britain in the fourth to eighth centuries was that it held together many of the strands of Christianity which today have become separated. The 'Celtic church'[5] had an Evangelical emphasis upon the scriptures and upon mission, a Catholic sense of the importance of incarnation and sacrament, a Pentecostal-charismatic experience of the work of the Holy Spirit, and an Orthodox vision of God as Trinity. My own journey of faith showed me that there was far more to God, his people and his mission on earth than the particular Christian stream labelled 'renewal' seemed able to express, and I was drawn to a community which seemed to be able to hold it all together.

Another important attraction was the idea of sharing our Christian journey with others in a relationship of encouragement and accountability. As I've described elsewhere,[6] I was in my 30s at the time, but I'd been in Christian leadership long enough to see people becoming driven or disillusioned, bullying or burned out. I remember commenting to a colleague that the model of ministry we operated seemed to depend on people being self-motivated self-starters. I could tick both boxes but I could also see how unhealthy that was.

A further draw was the realisation of remarkable similarities between the first millennium and the third. Anglo-Saxon men fought hard, then drank hard. Many of our town centres today are full of people doing exactly the same two things – but in reverse order! Yet into this violent and dangerous society came a vibrant expression of Christianity which transformed lives and permeated the entire culture. There had to be something to learn from that.

I picked up a copy of Ray Simpson's *Exploring Celtic Spirituality* during a holiday in Scotland. Once I started reading it, I couldn't put it down. On every page I turned, I learned something new, but no sooner had I taken it in than I felt as if I'd always known it. Suddenly the pieces of so many things I'd been thinking about were joining together. When I read at the end of the book that there was a community trying to live this spirituality out, I knew at once that I had to join them.

Unlike some of the experiments in Christian community in the 1970s, the Community of Aidan and Hilda is a *dispersed* community. This means that most of the members generally don't live very near each other, so they don't share everything in common under one roof, as did older monastic orders or some of the previous experiments in community. Other modern communities, such as the Iona Community, the Northumbria Community and the Franciscan Third Order, work in the same way. I discovered that in spite of this, and in spite of the fact that CA&H members sometimes only see each other once a year, if that, they have an extraordinarily strong sense of real community – a deeply held commitment to God and to one another expressed with a genuine personal warmth. Their common desire to grow in connection with God, and to connect God with the whole of life, results in a powerful connection with each other. Despite coming from different countries, cultures and settings, and from some pretty diverse church backgrounds, it is possible to see people only rarely and yet to enjoy a depth of relationship in Christ which many churches struggle to touch upon. What makes this possible?

Many present-day churches, whatever their denomination or structure, try to gather together a congregation and then, afterwards, to address the challenge of turning it into a community. Those operating on the parish system that grew up in the Middle Ages try to serve a geographical territory which often bears no relation to living patterns of local people. The two churches of my Anglican parish are divided by a six-lane road! Many of the Free Churches are defined by a particular theological standpoint – for example, adult baptism – and their members will travel significant distances to find a church which fits their beliefs. More recently founded churches or 'fresh expressions' of church are often defined by their style of worship, again tending to attract people who are willing and able to travel to find something which relates to them. What they all have in common is that they start by pulling a crowd (or trying to!) and then have to face the challenge of turning it into a community.

Celtic churches worked the other way round. They started as communities and then gathered wider congregations, which attached themselves to the communities and took on their values and practices. All of these churches were basically monasteries but, to understand them and unlock their potential for today, we need to abandon most of our preconceived ideas of what a monastery is like.

Let's look at one of the most famous Celtic monasteries, the seventh-century mixed community of men and women who were presided over by a remarkable woman called Hilda of Whitby. If you go to present-day Whitby, you'll find a town more interested in Dracula than Christianity, thanks to Bram Stoker's novel in which the world's most famous vampire lands in England at this north-eastern fishing town. High on the cliff-top above the town stand the iconic remains of the medieval monastery, a massive stone structure which speaks of power and awe, erected to pray for the soul of the Anglo-Norman nobleman who had it built. Whatever Hilda's monastery was like, and there are almost no remains, it was nothing at all like this.

Here's what it almost certainly was like. Imagine yourself cross-ing the wild and exposed North Yorkshire Moors, probably on a bracingly windy day, and, with a certain feeling of relief, coming in sight of the sea and your destination. What you see is neither a pillared cloister nor a tall stone spire but something that looks for all the world like a large village or a small town – and that is exactly what it is, a village of God. There are houses and animal sheds, workplaces and shops, and somewhere in the middle stands a wooden building which doesn't look much different from any of the others but is, in fact, the church. As you approach, you see not a high stone wall but a simple dry ditch encircling the village. This ditch serves a practical purpose in that it stops the animals from wandering away, but it has a symbolic purpose too. It reminds everyone that once they are inside the circle, the rules of the kingdom of heaven apply and everyone must seek to live by them. Within the village is a bewildering array of people. There are monks and nuns living under the disciplined and compassionate rule of life set up by Hilda. There are lay members of the community – men, women and children, single people and families – who follow the community rule less strictly. There are other Christians who live and work there, and probably also pagan visitors enjoying the hospitality of the community or seeking Hilda's practical wisdom while seeing what living Christianity looks like.

Three core elements bind this community powerfully together. First, there is the *Way of Life*, which in those days would have been called a Rule – a set of practices which everyone would have followed according to their particular level of commitment, designed to help them to follow the path of Christ and take on his character in day-to-day living. Second, there is the *rhythm of prayer*, the simple patterns of worship, intercession and Bible reading which punctuate the day and enable everyone consciously to connect with God and remember that every hour belongs to him. Third, there is the practice of *Soul Friendship*. Every member of the community has a Christian brother or sister whose task is to accompany them on their spiritual journey, listening to them and offering encouraging prayer and compassionate counsel. This care extends to ordinary Christians who simply live in this village of God, and it is also available to anyone, believer or pagan, who wants to draw near to the living God.

These are the three essential practices which are followed in a modern form by the Community of Aidan and Hilda and which enable this dispersed, international and interdenominational community to enjoy such a deep mutual commitment. Similar practices are followed by other dispersed Christian communities such as the Franciscan Third Order, mentioned earlier. The result is people who are growing Christians, deepening their connection with God and one another, and connecting God with the whole of life in a multitude of creative ways which advance the kingdom of God on earth.

Jeremiah 6:16 says this: 'Thus says the Lord: Stand at the crossroads, and look, and ask for the ancient paths, where the good way lies; and walk in it, and find rest for your souls.' For many years I have been a contributor to a popular series of daily Bible reading notes. I was invited to a meeting to explore a new range of publications which we might be able to get sold on the high street, aimed at the many people seeking practical spiritual guidance in their day-to-day lives. Most of the other people there were from new and emerging Christian communities, closely in touch with popular culture and discovering innovative ways to communicate and express their faith. I felt awkwardly out of touch. But as we talked, it became clear that I had been invited because of my links to Celtic spirituality and, as I explained about the core values and practices of the Community of Aidan and Hilda, people were attentive and interested. Many of these new communities have realised the need to find ways of helping their busy and active members to connect more deeply with God and each other. They are also sensing that there are first-millennium answers to their third-millennium questions.

The 24–7 Prayer movement began with a group of young people seeking God and finding far more than they imagined. Prayer led to mission, which led to a building and a group of people and the realisation that what they needed to sustain it was community. In their groundbreaking book *Punk Monk*, Andy Freeman and Pete Greig write that 'the reason for community is to help us follow Christ, to help others to live Christ-like lives'. They quote Jean Vanier, founder of the L'Arche communities, who said that 'the difference between community and a group of friends is that in a community we verbalise our mutual belonging and bonding'.[7] It is no surprise to find the 24–7 Boiler Room communities drawing heavily on Celtic models and inspirations for their way of life and rhythm of prayer.

It's not just radical new communities who are looking to our ancient roots for inspiration. On several occasions the Community of Aidan and Hilda has been involved in leading the reflective worship slot at the annual Spring Harvest event in Minehead, Somerset, attended by thousands of Christians from all over Britain. In 2009 we were invited to present a seminar entitled 'Developing your rule of life'. I arrived at Minehead to meet up with fellow Community members Penny Warren and David Cole, wondering what we had let ourselves in for. With some of the best-known Christian conference speakers in the country on hand, why would anyone want to come and listen to people they'd never heard of talking about a subject they probably knew nothing about? On top of that, we discovered we had been allocated a venue right on the fringe of the site which was not at all easy to find. Buoyed up by the thought that we would give our best shot to whoever turned up, however few, we busied ourselves working with the technical team to ensure that microphones and laptops were working properly and trying to grab a few minutes to pray.

With ten minutes to go, people started to come in. We smiled and tried to pretend we were perfectly relaxed. With five minutes to go, we noticed that the stewards were becoming a little agitated. Extra stacks of chairs were appearing and being hurriedly set out in rows as more and more people were arriving to sit on them. As start time arrived, nearly 200 people were packed into the venue, and for the next few days we could not move around the site without being asked further questions about what we'd shared in that one-hour seminar. People are clearly looking for ways to connect more deeply with God and to connect God with the whole of life, and the wisdom of our spiritual ancestors is speaking ever more clearly to them today.

In the following chapters we are therefore going to explore each of these three essential practices – a way of life, a network of soul friends, and a rhythm of prayer – to see how they can be adopted today in the lives of ordinary Christians and ordinary churches. After all, if following them has such a powerful and life-changing impact on individuals who belong to a dispersed community spread across the world, what might begin to happen if they were to be widely adopted by the members of local churches?

Chapter 2

Sharing a Way of Life

'Rules are mostly made to be broken,' said Douglas MacArthur, the famous World War II American general, 'and are too often for the lazy to hide behind.' When it comes to God, the apostle Paul was emphatic that human regulations are a waste of time and of no use in promoting spiritual growth (Colossians 2:20–23). So why on earth are we talking about following a Way of Life, which some Christian traditions call a Rule, and what on earth is one anyway?

Put simply, a Way of Life is a simple summary set of guidelines, outlining what it means in practice to live a God-centred life in a particular time or setting. Put another way, it's the 'To Do' list for how to connect with God and how to connect God with the whole of life. Notice that a Way of Life is context-sensitive. In other words, it may change from one place to another and one time to another. The Bible is our source book for everything God absolutely needs us to know. A Way of Life helps us apply what is in the Bible in practical ways. It will vary, however, according to our setting. The Way of Life of a traditional monastic community will have different emphases from that of the Community of Aidan and Hilda because it has to address how people are to live with each other under the same roof 24 hours a day for many years. The relational issues will be far more intense than those in an international and dispersed community or, indeed, those in a local church that has decided to adopt a Way of Life.

Ways of Life will also vary according to God's specific call and vision for different kinds of community. The Rule followed by the Boiler Room communities of the 24–7 movement highlights the practice of creativity as one of its six elements. This reflects something which has been integral to the movement from its beginnings and is, for them, a natural outflow of their foundational life of prayer. Writing it into the Rule ensures that it is never displaced or downgraded. The Order of Mission (TOM) was inaugurated by David Hope, the Anglican Archbishop of York in 2003, to do exactly what its name suggests. Its Way of Life, called 'Lifeshapes', is pragmatic and functional. Diane Kershaw of TOM describes it as 'a set of practical tools for missionary living that are grounded in biblical insights'.[8] There will, of course, be many overlaps between the way members of TOM live and the way members of a Boiler Room community live. Both are deeply rooted in scripture, but their respective Ways of Life reflect the different callings and journeys with God of these distinctive communities. Once again, this reflects and honours the principle of diversity among God's people and the recognition that, in our growth to maturity in God, one size does not fit all.

A Way of Life is one of the key elements of monastic life that bound together the early Christian communities, but there are powerful and compelling reasons to think that it is good and beneficial for all Christians and needs to be rediscovered today. Here are six of those reasons.

1 Living by a Way of Life is modelled in scripture

When the faith that we now call Christianity started, its followers were not known as Christians. Acts 11:26, describing the expansion of the church after the death of the first martyr, Stephen, and the conversion of a man called Saul of Tarsus, mentions that 'it was in Antioch that the disciples were first called "Christians"'. Before that, and continuing later in Acts, they were known simply as those who 'belonged to the Way' (9:2). No one is quite sure where this name originated but the *New International Dictionary of Christian Theology* draws the obvious conclusion that it emphasises how the message about Jesus also 'comprises a particular walk of life or way'. So, from the beginning, Christianity has always been not just about believing in Jesus but about expressing our belief by the way we live.

This is nothing new and goes right back to the roots of our faith to be found in the Old Testament. To be an Israelite, one of God's chosen people, was first and foremost a matter of birth – which is why those long lists of names in books such as Chronicles are so important. But it was more than that. You were born into a community (which grew into a nation) that was defined by its covenant with God. The terms of the covenant were very simple: 'I am the Lord your God, who brought you out of the land of Egypt, out of the house of slavery; you shall have no other gods before me' (Deuteronomy 5:6-7). This loyalty to God was then defined in the Law, the five books of Moses which make up the first part of our Old Testament. The Law was a huge body of material which, many scholars think, evolved over time, and by the time of Jesus it required specially trained teachers of the law to interpret and apply it. What were simple ordinary people in the second millennium BC to do? How could they be sure they were doing the right things to express their desire to love God with all their heart, soul and might (Deuteronomy 6:5)?

The answer is that from the very start there were simpler, shorter summaries of the Law which could be easily memorised and followed. The most famous are the Ten Commandments (Exodus 20:2-17; Deuteronomy 5:6-21). Many of us will be so familiar with the details of these that we will miss their larger implications. They provide a simple set of guidelines, in an often violent, vengeful and idol-worshipping world, for how to maintain loyalty to God, uphold family life and deal justly within society. They are a Way of Life for Israelites.

What's more, they are not the only example. At several other points in the Old Testament, particularly when many of the people were deported into exile in Babylon, we find similar checklists, usually with the same three emphases, to enable God's people to live faithful lives in their current situation.[9]

When we come to the New Testament we see Jesus bursting on to the scene with his explosive message that God's rule on earth is now at hand and that people should turn from their existing ways and put their trust in him (see Mark 1:15). Again we know that, just like the Old Testament Law of Moses, Jesus' teaching covered a huge variety of subjects. As he travelled around and people responded to his call to become his followers, they will have needed to know what would be involved. Mark frequently emphasises Jesus' role as a teacher but gives few instances of his in-depth teaching. It is Matthew, who almost certainly wrote his Gospel partly as an expansion of Mark, who describes what Jesus actually taught. 'When Jesus saw the crowds, he went up the mountain; and after he sat down, his disciples came to him. Then he began to speak, and taught them, saying...' (Matthew 5:1–2). What follows is one of the most famous sets of moral and spiritual instruction in human history. We call it the Sermon on the Mount (5:3—7:29).

The Sermon on the Mount has been an inspiration to millions of people down the centuries but it creates a lot of problems when you try to put it into practice. Jesus told his followers not to resist evildoers, to turn the other cheek, to give to those who demanded their property, and to go along with unreasonable demands (5:38–41). Not surprisingly, this has led to many ethical debates between Christians about how we should respond to crime and whether or not it is right to serve in the Armed Forces. One of the most intense instances was the dilemma faced by 20th-century German pastor, theologian and martyr, Dietrich Bonheoffer. Years ahead of his time, Bonhoeffer prophetically saw that 'the restoration of the church will surely come from a sort of new monasticism which has... a life lived according to the Sermon on the Mount'.[10] The challenge for him was how then to resist the appalling evil perpetrated by Adolf Hitler's Nazi regime in Germany, and Bonhoeffer came to the reluctant conclusion that the only way to prevent a greater evil was to participate in the lesser one of supporting the plot to assassinate Hitler.

Most of us will not face such intense dilemmas but, if we read the Sermon on the Mount closely and with a sincere desire to follow Jesus, we will find it hard to put some of it into practice. It will help us enormously to realise that Jesus was not sitting on a mountain uttering timeless moral truths into the air and leaving them to echo down the ages, to be applied unquestioningly in entirely different situations. He was addressing an audience of first-century Galileans living under Roman occupation, at least some of whom thought that if they started a war with the Romans, God would help them win it. A very important part of Jesus' teaching was that God's plans for Gentile pagans did not include being slaughtered in a holy war. The would-be followers of the Prince of Peace were to model radical peace-making, and it is this very specific situation that some of Jesus' harder sayings address.

This is not to say that the Sermon on the Mount does not speak to us today or that it does not have important things to tell us about how to deal with violence and oppression. My main point is that it is not trying to give a fully worked-out theology of war, government, crime and justice, but it is trying to give specific guidance on how to live as followers of Jesus in first-century Galilee. When Paul gives similar guidance on how to live faithfully as God's people in first-century Rome, he touches on the right of governments to use force to suppress evil (Romans 13:1–7). He is addressing different people in a different situation.

You might think that Paul would be the last person to ask about living by a Way of Life when so much of his teaching is about how Christians are free from the Old Testament laws and led instead by the inner guidance of the Holy Spirit. 'Did you receive the Spirit by doing the works of the law or by believing what you heard?' he pointedly demands of the Galatians (Galatians 3:2). Instead he urges them to 'live by the Spirit' and not to 'gratify the desires of the flesh' (5:16), and goes on to write the famous section describing the fruit of the Spirit (5:22–23). If that were all that Paul said, we might safely assume that he wanted his readers to be free from all the demands of the Old Testament law and expected that the inner guidance of the Holy Spirit would lead them to live in a God-pleasing way. But that is not the case. In this letter, as in many others, Paul goes on to spell out the sort of behaviour which goes with a God-pleasing life. The Galatians are told to avoid conceit, competition and envy (5:26), to restore wrongdoers with gentleness (6:1), to bear each other's burdens (v. 2) and to share what they have with those who teach them (v. 6).

It's sometimes easy to think that Paul is just dashing off random bits of good advice at the end of his letters, like a well-meaning parent sending children off on a school trip. In fact, what he says here is as carefully thought out as anything else he writes. Galatians was either the first or the second letter that Paul wrote. It was addressed to a church he had founded personally in an area that is now modern Turkey. After he had moved on, others had come into the church teaching that Gentile converts needed to take on the full package of Jewish beliefs and practices – including circumcision for the men – if they wanted to be regarded as true Christians. The church was thrown into turmoil. Paul's teaching about being 'justified' (declared to be in the right with God) solely as a result of Jesus' death on the cross, and his emphasis on the work of the Holy Spirit, was a direct response to this distortion of the good news, but so were the instructions on behaviour at the end of the letter. Mutual acceptance, support and forgiveness are not only the logical overflow of life based on God's gracious generosity, but were also the answer to a divided church in which one party was trying to enforce its code of behaviour on another. Remember that these were relatively new Christians. Paul was giving them a simple Way of Life to help them follow Christ day by day.

The same applies to Paul's other letter to new Christians, 1 Thessalonians. According to Acts 17:1–10, Paul had only spent a very short time leading the Thessalonians to faith and planting the church before he was evicted from the city. Imagine a church led by people who have only been Christians for about a month!

Chapters 4 and 5 of the letter are full of basic teaching on how to live as a Christian, aimed very specifically at people who, in the main, were ex-pagans who did not have the moral structure of the Old Testament to shape their behaviour. Paul deals with issues of work, sexual morality, relationships with those outside the church as well as within, and appropriate response to the work of the Spirit. Once again, what we have here is a Way of Life – a simple checklist for how to live a God-pleasing life in a pagan city in ancient Greece.

Paul does the same kind of thing at greater length in the letters to the Romans, Ephesians and Colossians. I hope the most important point is now clear, that living by a Way of Life is a thoroughly biblical thing to do. Scripture itself is full of examples of these simple summary sets of guidelines, laying out what it means in practice to live a God-centred life in a particular time or setting. That leads us neatly into the second reason why living like this is a good thing to do.

2 Living by a Way of Life is a good Christian practice

They say that the first time you do something new in a church, people greet it with dismayed cries of 'We've never done it that way before.' If you persevere and do it again, they'll be much happier because 'That's how we did it last year.' By the time you do it the third time, woe betide anyone who wants to change it again because 'That's how we've always done it!' My point is that most Christians – and, indeed, most people generally – don't have much sense of historical perspective. We tend to take for granted that the way we do things now is the way they've always been done.

Unless you're either a historian or an insomniac you probably won't have read a book called *The Ecclesiastical History of the English People* by the Venerable Bede. It's actually a lot better than it sounds, because it is the earliest history of how the gospel first came to the

British Isles, written less than a century after the Celtic evangelists, led by Aidan of Lindisfarne, had seen the conversion of the pagan Saxons. Bede describes the work of Cedd, one of the first Englishmen to be trained in the Christian community at Lindisfarne, who was sent as a missionary bishop to the people of Essex. According to Bede, Cedd 'gathered together a multitude of Christ's servants and taught them to observe the discipline of a Rule, so far as these rough people were capable of receiving it'.[11]

Here we see the seventh-century equivalent of an Alpha or Emmaus course: people have come to faith in Christ, so what do we do with them now? The question is still a valid one. Today we send them on a course, and then maybe another course. Cedd taught them to follow a simple Way of Life so that they would know what to do now that they were Christians. Notice that this was for new Christians. We often think of a Way of Life as being only for very committed people who either become monks or nuns or want to live like monks or nuns. Cedd teaches it as a good and life-giving practice for every Christian, right from the start.

3 Living by a Way of Life is a way of bringing God into the whole of life

I've heard preachers say that if Jesus isn't Lord of all, he isn't Lord at all. There's some truth in that, and one of our constant challenges as Christians is to keep in balance the fact that while God loves us and accepts us absolutely unconditionally, what we're called to offer in return is unlimited access to and ownership of every part of our lives. The problem, once again, is how we live this out in practice. We may not like to admit it, but many of us have probably had the experience of looking at someone else and thinking, 'How can they be a Christian and do *that*?' The attitude or action which shocks or offends us may not be a sign of hypocrisy on their part; they have simply never realised that their walk with God was meant to affect that particular area of their life. More positively, many of us will have had the experience of listening to a talk or reading a book and discovering that God was calling us to change in an area of life we had never thought about before. Yet still the challenge remains: what should I do now, and how am I going to keep it up when the next challenge comes along?

Living by a Way of Life goes a long way towards solving these problems by enabling us to keep track of our good resolutions. For years, management gurus have told us that good goals are SMART ones – Specific, Measurable, Achievable, Realistic and Time-bound. We know we ought to pray more, so we resolve to set aside a certain time each day to do so. We're challenged about how we handle our money and possessions, so we write into our Way of Life how we will organise our giving or manage our credit cards. We're told that Christians ought to be active in addressing the environmental crisis. Instead of feeling overwhelmed, we spend some time noting the specific steps we can take to begin to live more sustainably. Just over 25 years ago, Richard Foster wrote a book called *Money, Sex and Power*,[12] in which he challenged Christians to apply their faith to the three things which arguably influence our lives the most. Living by a Way of Life puts that challenge into practice by equipping us to address the whole of life and connect it with God.

4 Living by a Way of Life is a tool for managing choices

Choice is both a blessing and a curse. For people living in a dictatorship, the ability to choose is a luxury they can only dream about. Many of us living in the Western world have such a multitude of choices that they threaten to overwhelm us. In a large supermarket you can easily find over 100 different varieties of breakfast cereal. No wonder shopping takes so long! On a more serious level, many parents go through agonies trying to decide which school to send their child to or trying to meet the entrance criteria for the one they want. Freedom of choice and, with it, the culture of competition are not always a blessing when we simply want to do the right thing, especially where people we care about are involved. So what can we do to manage our daily choices?

Having a Way of Life means that we have already adopted a set of values and practices which we have thought about and which shape the way we live from day to day. It means that when we face choices and decisions, we are not starting from scratch every time or frantically praying for guidance because we haven't a clue what to do. A friend of mine is fortunate enough to be relatively well off. Like me, she believes that God allows people to have wealth but that they must use it wisely. For her, that means a commitment to generosity on the one hand (she sponsors the education of a child in Africa every year) and, on the other, a principle of seeking quality rather than extravagance in what she buys. Her Way of Life guides her through the whirlpool of choices created by our consumerist society in a way that honours God and cares for others.

5 Living by a Way of Life is a plan for a Christ-centred, Spirit-filled life

I highlighted in Chapter 1 how Paul said that the goal of his ministry was to 'present everyone mature in Christ' (Colossians 1:28). In his neighbouring letter to the Ephesians, he speaks about how everyone is to grow 'to maturity, to the measure of the full stature of Christ' (Ephesians 4:13). Once again, the big question is how we go about achieving maturity, and how we know when we have got there. Aim at nothing, the old saying goes, and you will be sure to hit it. If, as we saw above, living by a Way of Life is a way of bringing God into the whole of life, it follows that if we have a plan for doing this, we will also be putting Christ at the centre of our lives more and more, and living an increasingly Spirit filled life.

Another way of looking at it is to think of a Way of Life as being like a map for the Christian life. As you will know if you were ever taught traditional navigation with a map and compass, the first thing you need to be able to do is to pinpoint your own location on the map. Only then can you work out how to get to the place you're aiming for. People are sometimes put off the idea of adopting a Way of Life because they think it is only for very mature Christians who have travelled a long way on their spiritual journey. In fact, it's quite the opposite. If you don't look at the map before the journey starts, you won't be able to see the best route to your destination. In the end, it doesn't really matter where we are on the map, just as long as we've got it open and can find ourselves on it. That proves we're journeying with a purpose, and starting off in that way ensures that we will arrive at Christ-like maturity.

6 Living by a Way of Life is a response to grace, not a burden of works

When I talk about living by a Way of Life, someone nearly always starts looking worried. Sooner or later, they express the worry that this sounds like reducing Christianity to a set of rules, with all the underlying concerns about trying to earn God's favour by our own good works.

One of the reasons why the Community of Aidan and Hilda refers to a Way of Life rather than using the more traditional expression, a 'Rule of Life', is that, for some of us, the traditional language carries the baggage of authoritarian, hierarchical and legalistic forms of Christianity from which we want to escape. I find it even more worrying to see how easily even churches that stand strongly on the Reformation tradition of justification (being declared to be in right standing with God) by faith alone can start building up quite rigid and narrow rules about how Christians should behave.

Let me therefore say, clearly and unambiguously, that when Paul says, 'By grace you have been saved through faith, and this is not your own doing; it is the gift of God – not the result of works'

(Ephesians 2:8–9), I absolutely believe it. And when Paul asks the Galatians, 'Did you receive the Spirit by doing the works of the law or by believing what you heard?' (3:2), I absolutely believe that the second answer is the right one. Nevertheless, it is fascinating that this same Paul, who is so pre-eminently the apostle of God's grace, has no hesitation in describing what the Christian life is meant to look like, and spelling out, sometimes very bluntly, the kinds of activities that are both consistent with and contrary to that life.

I'm not much of a gardener – grass cutting is about the extent of my abilities – but I know from many people who are gardeners that if you want to make sure a young plant will grow well, you put a stick or frame next to it, to channel its growth in the right directions and stop it falling over. What we're trying to grow is the plant, not the frame. A Way of Life is simply an external structure which surrounds and supports our life in God. We depend utterly and absolutely on God's grace. We use everything we can to enable God's grace to achieve its goal in us – the development of a Christ-like person. Living by a Way of Life is a powerful and effective means to that end.

Developing a Way of Life

You can now see why living by a Way of Life is a good thing. How, then, do we go about developing one?

One way is to try to develop your own. Harold Miller offers some suggestions on how to do this in a little book called *Finding a Personal Rule of Life*.[13] He provides a useful grid in which to plot what we already do to express our Christian faith in the settings of our personal walk with God, meeting in groups, our family, our church, our daily prayer life and our wider activities. This is a good place to start, but, as we will see when we look at an example of a developed Way of Life below, there are many gaps.

Some churches work with the idea of a 'membership covenant'. I tried to create one of these some years ago. It was called 'Waymarks' and had six elements:

- Commitment to Christ
- An achievable pattern of prayer and Bible reading
- An achievable pattern of church attendance
- Planned giving
- Christian education and training
- Serving God through serving others

At the time, I did not have sufficient understanding of how to develop the idea further – not least because I lacked the skills of being a soul friend to someone, which I will explain in the next chapter. It was also very limited in scope and very church-focused rather than whole-life-focused. As a process, 'Waymarks' petered out, but there was sufficient interest at the time from people in our churches to encourage me that living by a Way of Life resonates with modern Christians, even if the idea is initially unfamiliar.

Devising your own Way of Life is not easy. The examples we looked at earlier, in the Bible, were created by law-givers, prophets, apostles and Jesus himself. Andy Freeman and Pete Greig describe the lengthy process by which the Way of Life of their communities developed: 'The Boiler Room rule hasn't emerged lightly. It has been the product of five years' hard work, hammered out on the anvil of real life and relationships and forged in prayer.'[14] So what do you do if you're convinced that it would be good for you or your church to follow a Way of Life? Is there a quicker way?

The great Celtic mission, which (most historians now agree) led to the conversion of England from the north southwards, began when Oswald, the Christian king of Northumbria, who had just regained his throne after a vital battle, invited a mission team from the great Christian community on the Scottish island of Iona, where he had been in exile, to bring the message of Jesus to his people. After an initial false start, the mission was led by a quietly-spoken Irishman called Aidan, who in AD635 founded a new community on the tidal island of Lindisfarne, a few miles across the sands from Oswald's stronghold at Bamburgh. Aidan, and his brother monks who accompanied him, will doubtless have continued to observe the Way of Life they had followed at Iona, which would have been known as the Rule of Columba. Aidan would then have taught it to others, and, as he was the recognised spiritual leader within the kingdom, it would soon have become known as the Rule of Aidan, with modifications to incorporate his own insights and way of teaching and living. It is significant that the historian Bede singles out Aidan's integrity of lifestyle for special praise: 'The best recommendation of his teaching to all was that he taught them no other way of life than that which he himself practised among his fellows.'[15] Bede goes on to highlight the way in which Aidan's own way of life became a model for others as they took on some of his distinctive personal disciplines of fasting and prayer.

One of Aidan's skills was to train and mentor others, and one of his greatest achievements was to spot the potential of a noblewoman who had embraced the monastic life. He appointed her leader of a community at Hartlepool, and after a few years she became abbess of one of the largest Christian communities in the north, at Whitby. Her name was Hilda. Such was her stature that we know more about her than almost any other woman in the entire first millennium. She was loved by ordinary people, trained five future bishops for the church, and was a counsellor to kings. Bede tells us that Hilda learned from Aidan the Way of Life he followed and taught, and this 'Way of Aidan' was followed in her communities. Bede also tells us that 'all who knew Hild… used to call her mother because of her outstanding devotion and grace', and that in later life she passed on to others what was 'taught by her own experience'.[16] As her spiritual and pastoral stature was recognised ever more widely, it is almost inconceivable that those who were taught by her would not have ended up following teaching which they thought of as the Way of Hilda.

I am not able to prove any of this conclusively, although the fact that many of the early Celtic monastic rules which have come down to us were not written by the people whose names they bear, but by their followers, suggests the kinds of processes by which these Ways of Life were handed on and developed. Nevertheless, what seems to have happened with Columba, Aidan and Hilda gave me the insight I needed for my own situation. If I was going to try to introduce a Way of Life into my own church, the place to start was with the one I already followed, road-tested not only in my own experience but also by members of the Community of Aidan and Hilda in many different settings across the world. At the same time, I was aware that it can sometimes be awkward and artificial simply to take an idea from elsewhere and try to incorporate it directly into another church community. I felt that if my congregation were to trust me down this new and unknown road, it would be helpful for them to hear it in a more familiar voice.

For that reason I decided to rewrite the Way of Life in my own words, adding a number of extra scripture references to earth it in the familiar language of the Bible, including small reflections and insights of my own, and changing the order of several of the elements in a way that felt more logical. All of this was done with the approval of Ray Simpson, the Community's founding Guardian, who offered much wise advice, encouragement and prayer support. Ray agreed with me wholeheartedly that if the Way of Life of a dispersed and international community were to take root in a local church, it would be right to adapt it where necessary, so that the end result bore a recognisable family resemblance to the original rather than being a clone.

The Way of Life

The original Way of Life of the Community of Aidan and Hilda can be found on the Community's website and is reproduced in full in Ray Simpson's book, *A Pilgrim Way*, which also provides an extensive commentary on how to put it into practice, along with a collection of spiritual wisdom, extraordinary in its breadth. At the end of this chapter is the version I have adapted for our own church setting. I have included the introduction, which recaps much of the material we have explored earlier in this chapter.

Putting it into practice

The first reaction many people have on reading this Way of Life for the first time is to feel overwhelmed and inadequate! This really shouldn't be too surprising when we remember what Christian living is all about – following a Jesus who said, 'Be perfect… as your heavenly Father is perfect' (Matthew 5:48), or the teachings of an apostle who told us to be 'imitators of God' (Ephesians 5:1). That's pretty challenging stuff, and the temptation is always to try to find a way of making these parts of the Bible mean something a bit less demanding. *But this is precisely where a Way of Life comes in!* A Way of Life is exactly what it says it is – a way of *life*, a plan to be worked out over many years, not something to be achieved overnight. As soon as we realise that, the pressure is off. The word 'perfect' that Jesus used also means 'complete' or 'fully developed' or having reached a goal. Our goal is to become mature in Christ, to connect as deeply as we can with God and to connect God as fully as possible with every part of our lives. The Way of Life gives us a plan to do that. It will take a lifetime to achieve it, but now we know not only where we're going but also how to get there, and all that matters is that we keep taking small steps forward.

Small steps are where we do best to begin. There's a lot to take in from this Way of Life. It's definitely a good idea to read it through many times as we pray about it and think about it, but I've also found it helpful, when introducing it to others for the first time, to break it down into simpler, smaller pieces. Having looked at the Ten Elements, I'll then encourage people to think about ten simple questions:

1 How am I seeking to grow in knowledge?

2 How do I experience companionship on my spiritual journey?

3 What is my personal rhythm of prayer, work and rest?

4 What are my guiding principles in my use of money and possessions?

5 What steps do I take to care for the environment?

6 How do I help others find healing?

7 What do I do to enable the Holy Spirit to guide me?

8 How do I support others through prayer?

9 How do I show welcome and hospitality to other people?

10 How do I help others to find faith in Jesus?

These questions do not capture everything in each of the elements but they provide a place to start. The first exercise in drawing up a personal Way of Life is to write down everything you are already doing in response to each of the questions. Many people will immediately be able to write something, sometimes quite a lot, under seven or eight of the headings. This, by the way, often brings a huge sense of relief and encouragement. We suddenly realise that we are already making greater progress in our journey with God than we thought. Immediately the Way of Life has brought encouragement to our Christian lives. I never cease to be amazed by the number of people who feel that the measure of a good sermon is that they come out feeling 'challenged'. Challenge is good when we need to make progress and we've got stuck, but I've yet to meet anyone who has come to grief as a result of receiving too much encouragement. Feeling that we are actually getting somewhere is often the biggest spur to pressing on further.

Inevitably, though, there will be some areas of the Way of Life where we draw a blank, and this reveals the gaps in our Christian learning and experience which need to be addressed. They will vary from person to person or according to the kind of Christianity we see practised around us. For many, the idea of having a soul friend is entirely new, not least because, along with a Way of Life, it has rarely been practised in the mainstream church for over a thousand years. For others, the idea of 'healing the land' is new. For others, integrating care for creation into their spirituality is still a new concept, despite the progress the church has made in this area in the last ten years. Wherever the gaps are, they need to be filled, but filled wisely. When confronted by a blank on the page, I frequently advise people in the first instance to make it their personal commitment to find out more about this particular area and then to identify one step they can take towards expressing it in their life. A Way of Life is something which should be reviewed regularly, so it will be possible at a future stage to be more specific.

This principle of keeping things small and simple is vitally important. My first soul friend wisely warned me against writing what he wryly described as 'a heroic list' of things that I could do to express each of the ten elements. With a little reflection, most of us can easily think of lots of extra commitments we might take on, but there is always a danger that we will simply lock ourselves into a cycle of failure, anxiety and guilt. The most important step is always the next one. When we've taken it – and not slipped – we can work out what comes after it.

I will write more about working out a personal Way of Life in the final chapter. I hope you will have realised already that the ten elements can be worked out in as many different ways as there are people living them. The literally vital, that is to say, life-giving dimension is working out what God is calling each of us individually to do at this moment in time. That process of discernment will be strongly shaped by our own personality. Some of us like big challenges and may overreach ourselves. Others of us are afraid of commitment or failure, so we may find it hard to begin the process. This is why we all need someone to walk the journey with us. That person is called a soul friend and they are the subject of the next chapter.

Way of Life

Introduction

Living by a Way (or 'Rule') of Life is commonly associated with the spiritual discipline taken on by monks and nuns in religious orders. In fact the practice of setting out the key elements of what it means to live as the people of God in a particular time and setting is well-established in the Bible and the early church. The Ten Commandments (Exodus 20) given to Moses summarise how God wanted the Israelites to live. The Sermon on the Mount (Matthew 5—7) taught by Jesus shows how he wanted his disciples to live, especially in the setting of first-century Palestine. Most of Paul's letters contain practical teaching on how to live the Christian life for his mixed Jew-Gentile churches in Roman cities. The English historian Bede tells us that when the Celtic missionary, Bishop Cedd, worked among the East Saxons, he 'taught them to observe the discipline of a Rule, so far as these rough people were capable of receiving it' (Bede, *The Ecclesiastical History* III.22).

Adopting a Way of Life is about seeking to live responsibly by bringing God into every area of our lives. The pace of 21st-century life confronts us with constant choices and demands which leave many people feeling exhausted and overwhelmed. By contrast, Jesus promised 'life to the full' (John 10:10, NIV). He spoke of taking on 'his yoke' but promised that through it we would find rest for our souls (Matthew 11:28–30). Living by a Way of Life therefore is not about legalistic rules which can cause further guilt, but rather about having God-given guidelines which allow us to say no to what is not essential in order to flourish and find freedom by doing what really matters. Christianity is about grace, not law, what God has done for us rather than what we have to do for God. Paul wrote, 'I died to the law, so that I might live to God. I have been crucified with Christ; and it is no longer I who live, but it is Christ who lives in me. And the life I now live in the flesh I live by faith in the Son of God, who loved me and gave himself for me' (Galatians 2:19–20). A Way of Life shows us what this Christ-filled life looks like in practice.

Three Basic Principles

Most early Christian communities were self-supporting and centred on people who were single. Their Way of Life was built on the traditional monastic vows of poverty, chastity (practised as celibacy), and obedience. A Way of Life was however always open to adaptation to fit changing circumstances. Most 21st-century people have families and working lives so flexibility is essential, and these vows are best understood today as guiding principles rather than strict rules. Our three foundational principles are therefore defined as *simplicity*, *purity* and *obedience*.

Simplicity
Jesus said, 'Seek first for the kingdom of God and his righteousness, and all these things [food and clothing] will be given to you as well' (Matthew 6:33). The essence of simplicity is to put the priorities and values of God's kingdom first in every area of life. This leads us to regard all that we have as gifts not as possessions, to be used as God guides us, and to trust that God will provide for our essential needs.

Purity
Jesus said, 'Blessed are the pure in heart, for they will see God' (Matthew 5:8). The essence of purity is being open before God in all our thoughts and feelings, including our sexuality. We show love, openness and generosity to all people following

the example of Christ, but reserve the sexual expression of love for a lifelong partner of the opposite sex. We honour marriage, respect those who choose to remain single, and affirm those for whom this area of life is a struggle.[17]

Obedience
Jesus said, 'Those who want to save their life will lose it, and those who lose their life for my sake will find it' (Matthew 16:25). The essence of obedience is the joyful abandonment of ourselves to God, giving up our will for his in the service of others. The root of obedience is therefore in learning to listen to God to learn his ways. We also give due respect to those whom God has placed in positions of leadership or seniority in church, family, the workplace and public life.

One Essential Practice: Soul Friendship

The early church in these islands and elsewhere practised the ministry of 'soul friendship'. A soul friend is a mature Christian who is in sympathy with our Way of Life, and who helps us to discern and respond appropriately to God's will, grow in maturity, responsibility and wholeness, and to deepen our relationship with God. Our soul friend helps us to work out our personal application of the Way of Life, reviews it with us at regular intervals, and is a companion to us on our spiritual journey.

Ten Core Elements

1 Lifelong Learning
2 Journeying with God
3 A Rhythm of Prayer, Work and Re-creation
4 Simple Lifestyle
5 Celebration and Care for Creation

1 Lifelong Learning

Jesus said, 'Take my yoke upon you, and learn from me... you will find rest for your souls' (Matthew 11:29). The definition of a disciple is one who learns.

We learn from the Bible and from creation. At the heart of our Way of Life is learning from God through daily Bible reading, and also through study, meditation, and any other means of creative engagement with the scriptures. The Bible also urges us to consider God's creation and to draw lessons from what we see there.

We learn from other people and from our life experiences. In particular we seek to learn from the lives and examples of the Celtic saints – the founders of the church in our islands, and from people of all ages whose example illuminates our Way of Life. We celebrate the lives of these saints and regard them as our companions and encouragers (Hebrews 11:1—12:2). Since all truth is God's truth we seek to increase our knowledge and understanding of all things which are life-enhancing and enrich our God-given personalities and gifts. We seek to grow in knowledge not for its own sake but that we may live more wisely and fully.

2 Journeying with God

We regard the Christian life as a journey and, like St Paul, we 'press on toward the goal... of the heavenly call of God in Christ

Jesus' (Philippians 3:14). We meet with our soul friend at least three times a year to share with them the progress we are making or the difficulties we are facing. They help us to discern what God is doing in our lives at the present time and where he might be leading us. Our soul friend is not however expected to act as our pastor, counsellor, spiritual director, or confessor unless we choose to seek out a person who has those specific gifts.

We regard two particular practices as important in helping us on our journey with God.

- Regular retreats: A retreat is an opportunity for quiet and reflection with God. Individual circumstances and lifestyles mean that this will be worked out in different ways, but it is vital that we take such time regularly. This may take the form of a designated 'quiet day', or we may only be able to set aside a period of a few hours. An annual retreat away from home is encouraged if at all possible.

- Pilgrimage: The Bible is full of people making journeys. The Celtic missionaries to Britain were adventurous travellers. Pilgrimage is about visiting significant places and seeking new experiences which will stimulate and inspire us on our journey with God. We visit, reflect, and pray at places which are part of our spiritual heritage, such as Lindisfarne and Iona, and places which have become significant to our own spiritual history. When we are able to, we take these opportunities to travel as an outward reminder that God is always on the move and we are called to follow where he leads us.

3 A Rhythm of Prayer, Work and Re-creation

- **Prayer**: The life of Jesus was fuelled by prayer and he taught the need to pray always (Luke 18:1). We commit ourselves to a regular pattern of daily prayer, alone or with others. Ways of praying will vary according to our personality but we affirm and encourage every kind of prayer from silent contemplation to celebratory praise. Set forms of prayer can be provided, as can guidance about how to establish and deepen our personal prayer life.

- **Work**: Jesus spoke frequently about work (for example, Luke 12:42–43). God intended from the beginning that human beings should engage in beneficial work (Genesis 2:15). We therefore welcome work as a gift from God and seek to engage in it whether through paid employment, the necessary tasks of daily life, or other constructive activities. Work involving values or practices which conflict with our Way of Life should be avoided as much as possible, but we seek the presence of God in every task, even unattractive ones. If we are unemployed or unclear what our work should be, we seek advice and guidance. We seek to resist pressures to overwork because it misuses time which should rightfully be given to God, others, or ourselves.

- **Re-creation**: Jesus taught that 'the Sabbath was made for humankind' (Mark 2:27) because God himself rested at the end of creation (Genesis 2:1–3). In the Old Testament even the land had a Sabbath rest every seventh year (Leviticus 25:1–4). Since time spent in rest and recreation is as essential as time spent in prayer and work, we build regular time for restoration and renewal of body, mind and spirit into our personal Way of Life.

4 Simple Lifestyle

Jesus said, 'You cannot serve God and wealth. For where your treasure is, there your heart will be also' (Matthew 6:24, 21). He also encouraged us to trust that God will always give us our daily bread (Matthew 6:11). We seek to be open and accountable before God (and, if appropriate, our soul friend) for the way we use our money and possessions, handle our time and activities, and the quality of our relationships and hospitality. We are conscious that we are stewards, not owners of these things, and we are ready to make them and ourselves available to others as God guides us.

Faced with global poverty and environmental crisis we seek to 'live simply that others may simply live'. This will mean different things for different people and we do not judge one another. We also enjoy and celebrate the good things God gives us and understand that there is a time to feast as well as to fast. We seek to order our possessions, activities and relationships in a way which frees us to be fully attentive to God, others, and ourselves, and we seek to get rid of those things which overload or clutter our lives. Our clothing and surroundings should reflect our God-given individuality, expressing beauty while rejecting extravagance. We also stand against the spirit of materialism by practising hospitality wherever possible and by committing to proportionate and generous financial giving.

5 Celebration and Care for Creation

Jesus called himself 'the light of the world [literally, the *kosmos*]' (John 8:12), and John declares that 'all things came into being through him' (John 1:3). There are many stories of the Celtic saints and other holy people living in harmony with wild creatures. We affirm that God's creation is essentially good, but is corrupted and damaged by the effects of human sin and the influence of the spiritual powers of evil. We believe that creation reveals the glory of God (Psalm 19:1) so we celebrate creation and seek ways to meet with and learn from God through it. We likewise seek to be environmentally aware, living in a way which respects and cares for God's creation and which stands against those values and practices that continue to damage it.

6 Healing of People, Relationships, Communities and Places

Jesus said, 'The Spirit of the Lord has anointed me to bring good news to the poor, to proclaim release to the captives and recovery of sight to the blind, to let the oppressed go free, to proclaim the year of the Lord's favour' (Luke 4:18–19). Paul wrote that 'through him God was pleased to reconcile to himself all things, whether on earth or in heaven, by making peace through the blood of his cross' (Colossians 1:20). St Irenaeus (second century) said, 'The glory of God is a human being fully alive.' In the name of Christ and through his power we pursue wholeness in body, mind and spirit for ourselves and for others. We seek to be peacemakers between estranged individuals and in divided communities. We also pray for the 'healing of the land' in places polluted by human sinfulness (2 Chronicles 7:14).

7 Openness to the Holy Spirit

Jesus told his disciples, 'When the Spirit of truth comes, he will guide you into all the truth' (John 16:13). He also spoke of the Spirit as the wind which blows wherever it chooses (John 3:8). Some Celtic Christian missionaries had such faith in the leading of the Spirit that they were willing to put to sea in small coracles, and go where the wind took them! Whether as a gentle breeze or a wild wind we seek the same kind of openness to the leading of the Spirit. We cultivate a willingness to let God move us beyond where we are comfortable and into what is new or unfamiliar.

The New Testament gift of prophecy has an important part to play in this. This is the spiritual gift of being able to receive insights from God which build up, encourage, console, guide or challenge, either for ourselves or for others. Paul encourages all Christians to desire this gift (l Corinthians 14:1). Such insights must be carefully weighed (1 Thessalonians 5:20–21) and learning to listen to God is a skill which requires time to develop. We seek to cultivate an inner stillness which can distinguish the voice of God from all the other 'voices' and influences within us. We also listen for God's voice through Scripture and through his creation.

8 Overcoming Evil Through Intercessory Prayer

Jesus understood his ministry to be a conflict between the kingdom of God and the spiritual powers of darkness (John 12:31; Luke 11:14–20). We recognise the reality of this unseen dimension and the ongoing warfare between the spiritual forces of good and evil (Ephesians 6:10–13). Prayer is a key weapon in this struggle (Ephesians 6:18) as we pray both for God's will to be done on earth as it is in heaven, and to be delivered from evil (Matthew 6:9–13). To pray in this way for people, places and situations is intercession. In doing so we do not project on to the unseen dimension things for which human beings need to take responsibility but we do seek to discern the spiritual influences at work there. Intercession is always related to positive action because our ultimate goal is to 'overcome evil with good' (Romans 12:21).

9 Cultivating Unity

Jesus said, 'I will draw all people to myself' (John 12:32), and prayed that his disciples, both then and now, 'may all be one' (John 17:20–21). Paul taught that we should all regard ourselves as members of the one body of Christ (1 Corinthians 12:12). The church today is marred by divisions between Eastern and

Western traditions, Protestants and Roman Catholics, and many other smaller splits. In the Celtic period the distinctive features of these different strands of Christianity were still woven together. The early church in Britain had the emphasis on Scripture and mission reflected today by Evangelicals, the emphasis on incarnation and sacraments reflected by Catholics, and the emphasis on the Spirit and the Trinity reflected by Pentecostals and the Orthodox tradition. It held in balance both the contemplative and the active life. The Celtic missionaries also adapted themselves to the culture, patterns and practices of the society they sought to reach for Christ. Aidan rejected anything which would make him superior or separate from the people. Hilda was regarded as a spiritual mother by many ordinary people.

Our first expression of unity is by making it a priority to worship and meet regularly with the other members of our own church fellowship. We also seek to welcome all Christians as fellow travellers with Christ, to express solidarity with them by actions as well as words, and to emphasise the things which unite us while we seek to overcome those which still divide us. We seek to cultivate solidarity with all people in everything except sin and to value and affirm what is good in all people and cultures. We seek to identify and remove attitudes and practices which create barriers between church and people. We act to overcome divisions based on gender, colour, or social status, wherever we find them.

10 Sharing Jesus and Justice

The last command Jesus gave to his followers was to 'make disciples of all nations' (Matthew 28:19–20) as the final stage of God's 'plan for the fullness of time, to gather up all things in Christ, things in heaven and things on earth' (Ephesians 1:10). The reason we are called to live in united community is 'that the world may believe' (John 17:21). An essential goal of our Way of Life, therefore, is to develop a disciplined spirituality which will make us effective witnesses for Christ. Centres of Christian community like Iona and Lindisfarne were mission bases for the spread of the gospel in the British Isles. Leaders like Aidan, Hilda, Cuthbert, Columba, David and Patrick made Christ known to others through words and actions wherever they went. They shared the gospel in ways which respected and began from the existing culture and beliefs of their hearers.

All Christians are empowered by the Holy Spirit to be witnesses (Acts 1:8), so motivated by the love of Christ (2 Corinthians 5:14) we seek to share our faith wherever God gives us an opportunity, taking time to listen to others before we speak. We seek to be led by the Spirit into new ways of sharing Christ which fit the culture in which we live, and to be open to demonstrations of the Spirit's power through prayer for healing and prophetic insights.

By speaking the truth prayerfully and in love we also seek to introduce God's peaceful rule wherever material or spiritual powers have taken his place. Following the example of Jesus, we also seek to minister to, and speak for, those oppressed by poverty and injustice (Matthew 11:2–5). The Celtic missionaries actively sought to bring a Christian influence to bear upon people in power to cause them to act justly and to open wider doors for the gospel. We seek to work with all people of good will in positions of influence so that our nations may reflect the values of the kingdom of God.

Chapter 3

Journeying with a Soul Friend

When I was studying theology and training to become a minister, one of my friends was a former journalist. She still did some radio work and one day she organised a live interview in front of an audience with the bestselling novelist Susan Howatch. The interview included short readings from her novels and I was invited to be one of the readers. After listening to the interview, I thought the least I could do was to read one of her novels in full.

Susan Howatch's first success was with a series of 'family saga' novels in the 1970s and early '80s. She then found herself on a spiritual search which drew her into the Christian faith. This inspired her to write a new and ultimately even more successful series of books, the six 'Starbridge' novels, set at different significant periods in the life of the Church of England in the 20th century. That may not sound very exciting stuff, but remember it's in the hands of a bestselling popular novelist with a gift for complicated plots and high-octane psychological dramas. 'Isn't that a bit lowbrow?' said a disapproving bishop when I told him what I was reading. I wonder if he knew how much he sounded like one of her characters! Imagine a long line with *War and Peace* at one end and a holiday blockbuster at the other and you'll have to make up your own mind about where these novels belong, but I ended up reading all six and they got me thinking.

The first novel, *Glittering Images*, is about a young and apparently very successful Cambridge University clergyman, Charles Ashworth, who is sent by the Archbishop of Canterbury in 1937 to investigate the unusual and potentially scandalous domestic arrangements of a prominent and controversial bishop. As he becomes increasingly entangled, the events bring to the surface his own cupboard-full of dark secrets, triggering a life-shattering emotional and spiritual crisis. Ashworth goes to recover at a monastery that he has used previously for retreats, only to find that the benign abbot, his usual undemanding spiritual confidant, has been replaced by the far more formidable Father Jonathan Darrow. Tall, austere and disturbingly perceptive, Darrow takes control of the crisis and, step by step, enables Charles to deal with and escape from his own distorted and damaging 'glittering image'. He is the ultimate 'spiritual director', authoritative yet compassionate, challenging but deeply caring, psychologically skilled yet spiritually perceptive. He is further assisted by having gifts of healing and an ability to perceive others' thoughts! (You'll have to read the second novel, *Glamorous Powers*, to find out that he has weaknesses too!)

Jon Darrow caught my imagination. I'm not sure that his unerringly accurate ability to read people and situations exists outside fiction, but I wondered what it would be like to meet someone like him. On the one hand, it would be bound to prove deeply unsettling. Like Charles, we all have difficult bits of our lives which we keep covered up because we don't want anyone else to see them, but they would not stay hidden for long from someone like Darrow – even if he did not use his special gifts. On the other hand, it might well be a massive relief to talk to someone like that. Openness about anything would be much easier because of the complete absence of condemnation and the knowledge that we were speaking with someone whose only concern was our own well-being, who had the skill to help us move towards that well-being. Nevertheless, I was left wondering whether such people really exist in real life and, if they do, whether anyone except a tiny minority of exceptionally mature and gifted Christians ever begin to become so skilled in helping and supporting others.

What Jon Darrow was doing for Charles Ashworth is, in a very dramatic and highly charged way, another example of what this book is all about – helping people to connect more deeply with God and to connect God with every part of their life. It's what we aim for as individuals but it is never something we can do on our own. How, then, do we go about creating the kind of community in which it can happen?

For many churches the answer has been to get people together in groups and on courses like Alpha, Emmaus and many others. There are many benefits to this approach but, as I indicated in Chapter 1, it can never be the whole solution, not least because of the fact that, even in churches with very good group structures, there are always lots of people who do not get involved in groups. A more traditional approach has been to have a programme of visiting church members. 'A home-going minister makes church-going people' is one old maxim I've heard. A previous minister of my church dedicated an entire year to visiting every single home in the parish. By my reckoning that means he must have visited an average of five homes every day! That was in the 1960s and it certainly did have some impact at the time. But what about now? To do that in my area today, you would need to be able to speak about 30 languages, there would be no reply from at least half the homes, and you could expect anything from embarrassment to outright hostility from a substantial proportion of the people who did open the door. Even among those of us who are Christians, the last thing most of us want in our busy lives is an unexpected visitor, even if it's the minister of our church.

Yet the personal, individual approach is still very important. The first church where I worked after college put a high value on helping people discover and use their God-given gifts. We used a course developed by Dr C. Peter Wagner, one of the pioneers of the study of church growth at Fuller Seminary in California. The process involved a self-assessment questionnaire, a group exercise and, finally, a personal interview. As I took people through the process, I noticed that, although it was a lot more scientific than anything I had ever seen before, the real work was in the interpretation of the results, talking and listening with the participants. There was also a danger that it would simply become an exercise in slotting people into vacancies on rotas, so I started to ask other questions as well.

'What are your hopes for this church?' was one of them. Another was, 'Is there anything you would especially like to do for God or the church, which you have never been asked or given the opportunity to do?' These questions would often open up a new dimension of conversation and I would frequently come away feeling that I had engaged on a deeper level with the person, that I now knew more about them and their walk with God and had been able to offer them some encouragement in it.

Despite what I say about the importance of helping individuals in their walk with God, I still think that courses and small groups are useful too. Nevertheless, as I kept seeing, there is enormous value in talking with people one-to-one about what God is doing in their lives. The problem is providing an easy context for that to happen. A few years after I came to London, someone pointed me towards a possible way forward.

Back in the 1990s, the vicar of a large Anglican church in Essex, Wallace Benn, had been inspired by the work of a 17th-century English Puritan minister called Richard Baxter. In his classic book *The Reformed Pastor*, first published in 1656 and still in print today, Baxter describes his work among the 2000 residents of the town of Kidderminster, which resulted in the majority of them becoming genuinely committed Christians in both their personal faith and the way they lived their lives. The key to this was not Baxter's preaching but his practice of going from house to house in order to talk to people individually about how to live as Christians. Wallace Benn tried to do a similar thing, first with a youth group and then with a whole church.[18] He told the whole congregation that he would invite them in turn to come and see him, to help him get to know them, but that he would also ask them how they were getting on as Christians. He reported that many people had found this process extremely helpful.

I read an article about the Benn and Baxter approach in which it was described as a 'spiritual MOT'. The idea immediately caught my imagination and in 2003 I introduced it among my two congregations. They were very positive about it but made the good point that the danger of a 'spiritual MOT' was that you might fail it! We decided that calling it a 'spiritual health check' sounded a lot less threatening. Wallace Benn had worked out quite a detailed process of questioning when he met with people and, while I decided that his list was not exactly what I wanted to use, it did seem wise to have a structure to the conversation. Consequently the spiritual health check became part of my first attempt to work out a Way of Life in a local church setting – the 'Waymark' scheme described in the previous chapter. The visits went well, all things considered, although I think one or two of the participants were a little bemused at times. The problem was that it was all very prescriptive. I had five or six different areas to talk about, with a good idea of the outcome I was looking for, but I was never entirely clear in my own mind how the conversation was going to continue after the first visit. It was an interesting experiment, but it did not continue because I was not yet sure where I was going with it.

So let's jump to the present day. Shirley is a member of my church who keeps a regular journal. With her permission I quote an excerpt from it:

> When Soul Friendship was first offered in my church I was seriously hesitant, but I did accept it and on 19 May 2010 I met my Soul Friend for the first meeting. In preparation [Shirley had not been asked to prepare: this was something she herself decided to do] I had made a list of the times when God was clearly in my life, and it was so nice to talk about these times and to have someone listen with interest. From that one single meeting I wanted to write and to start a journal. I wanted to write about the day I met God… and through my writing I now understand what I must do.

In the mid 1990s Shirley had an overwhelmingly vivid and powerful encounter with Jesus as she was walking to work one day. It brought her faith dramatically to life, but, until she had this regular opportunity to reflect, she had never been able to work out what God wanted her to do as a result. As she puts it, 'I simply want to show kindness to people', and that kindness specifically includes trying in a gentle and friendly way to introduce them to Jesus. Now in her 70s, Shirley is one of the keenest helpers on our Alpha courses and has a wonderful ability to befriend people across the generations. She brings a warmth and joyfulness wherever she goes.

In case this all sounds a bit too good to be true, and another gooey Christian 'success' story, there's something else you need to know. Shirley has also been a full-time carer for her husband, who has a degenerative brain condition and cannot be left alone for more than a few minutes. As you will know if you have experienced anything like this, sleepless nights are a regular occurrence, as is a constant and worrying need for vigilant care. Yet Shirley expresses nothing but thanks to God for every day of a long and happy marriage, and when she says she knows joy and peace most of the time, you are inclined to believe her.

Look at what is happening here. Shirley has been helped into a process of reflection which has enabled her to discern more clearly God's work in her life and to become more sensitive to the promptings of his Spirit. This has the twofold effect of helping her to draw on God's strength in her very difficult personal circum-stances and, at the same time, respond to a clear vocation to reach out with Christ's kindness to other people. All the glory belongs to God, but both Shirley and I can see that engaging in the supportive spiritual companionship known as Soul Friendship has helped her in numerous ways to connect more deeply with God and to connect God with her life and the lives of others.

What do we mean by Soul Friendship?

Out of the mists of time, from a borderland between history and legend, we hear the powerful voice of a strong woman. According to St Brigid, one of the greatest Celtic saints of Ireland, 'a person without a soul friend is like a body without a head'. The expression used is the evocative Gaelic term *anamchara*. *Cara* means 'friend' and *anam* means 'soul'. Theologians argue about precisely what the Bible means by the soul (many Christians think of it as the non-physical part of us which lives on when we die), but the word is used here to mean the whole person – the mind and the spirit which animate the body. My *anamchara* is the person who will be a friend to every part of me and every part of my life.

The ministry of the *anamchara* was one of the distinctive and powerful features of Celtic Christian spirituality, in Ireland and wherever else it spread. One of the greatest English saints in the Celtic tradition is Cuthbert, who ministered in Scotland and England in the seventh century. Cuthbert received his own personal call from God in a vision that he saw on the night that Aidan died. As a young man he had been a keen, strong athlete and he took this physical resilience and stamina into Christian ministry, often travelling for weeks at a time to visit the most distant and inaccessible settlements in Northumbria where no one else would go. In later life Cuthbert felt a strong call to spend time alone with God in a solitary life as a hermit, but such was his reputation as a pastor that people kept coming back to find him. Bede describes what happened when they met him:

> They confessed their sins, confided in him about their temptations, and laid open to him the common troubles of humanity they were labouring under... They were not disappointed. No one left unconsoled, no one had to carry back the burdens he came with. Spirits that were chilled with sadness he could warm back to hope again... To men beset with temptation he would skilfully disclose all the wiles of the devil.[19]

Something very special was going on here. In earlier life Cuthbert had a reputation as an evangelist and teacher. He showed his love for the people of the north-east by putting himself at risk to go and find them in the obscure places where they lived. But this was something different. People were coming to find Cuthbert in order to share with him the deepest and sometimes darkest places of their lives. Bede suggests that they were met by unconditional love and a willingness to listen without judging, coming from a man who was known to dedicate himself to seeking God's face and God's ways. They felt able to bare their souls because they were doing so with a man who had proved himself to be the friend of their souls.

Another great Celtic soul friend was Hilda of Whitby, whom we have met already. Through Hilda's gift of soul friendship, the emerging English language gained the first poet whose name we know – Caedmon.

Caedmon lived and worked as a cowherd in Hilda's great village of God at Whitby. A common feature of the culture of Celtic and Anglo-Saxon England was that in the evenings people would gather round the fire to take it in turns to sing songs and tell stories. Caedmon was a shy man and would always find an excuse to slip out when it came close to being his turn to perform. One night he went back to mind the cattle and, having gone to sleep, he had a dream. God appeared to him in the form of a man and asked him to sing something. Caedmon made his usual excuses, but the visitor insisted and told him that he must sing about God's creation. Caedmon burst spontaneously into song.

In the morning, not even he could keep this quiet for long and he was taken to Hilda, who listened carefully to his story. To test and develop his gift, she set him some homework. Caedmon was read a biblical story and told to come back with another song, which he duly did. Hilda instructed the monastic community to receive him as a full member and to teach him the scriptures so that he could put them into songs and poems in English which ordinary people could understand.

We only have a fragment of that first song, known as 'Caedmon's Hymn':

> *Now let me praise the keeper of Heaven's kingdom,*
> *The might of the Creator, and his thought,*
> *The work of the Father of glory, how each of wonders*
> *The Eternal Lord established in the beginning.*
> *He first created for the sons of men*
> *Heaven as a roof, the holy Creator,*
> *Then Middle-earth the keeper of mankind,*
> *The Eternal Lord, afterwards made,*
> *The earth for men, the Almighty Lord.*

Scholars widely agree that this is the oldest written poem in the English language. Without Hilda's gift of soul friendship, which built Caedmon's confidence in his God-given gift, we might never have had it at all. We can only guess how many other ordinary people came to this influential woman to find a compassionate listening ear and keen insight into the work of God in their lives. Judging by the accounts we have of them, the Celtic saints were formidable and sometimes quite scary people, but common to them was a love for ordinary people and a willingness to step down to meet them on their own level in order to aid the work of God in their lives. One of the most striking stories about Aidan concerns the king's gift to him of a horse. The gift was well intentioned, designed to make the spiritual leader of the kingdom more mobile and available to a wider number of people, but that was not how Aidan saw it. The first time he met a beggar, he gave away the horse in order to relieve his poverty. When the king challenged him, Aidan famously asked him whether he thought the son of a mare was more important than the son of a man. The symbolism of the story is striking. As well as compassion for the poor, Aidan demonstrated in the most dramatic way possible that he would always prefer to walk alongside other people than look down upon them from above. That, in essence, is what Soul Friendship is all about.

You might wonder where the Celtic Christians got this idea, since it was so distinctive to their way of living the Christian life. We saw in the first chapter that one of the many differences between the first-millennium church and later developments was that it was monastic in its core values and practices, and this is where the idea of Soul Friendship comes from.

The monastic movement was probably the first radical reform movement in Christian history. For the first few centuries, Christianity was a minority religion, although a growing one, in a Roman world which had no love for its values and which, from time to time, actively persecuted its members. There were no social advantages to being a Christian. In the early fourth century, everything changed when the Emperor Constantine embraced Christianity. Suddenly Christianity became fashionable and, if you wanted to get on under the new regime, it made sense to be known as a Christian. Social Christianity had begun. Rather than being delighted at this apparent victory for their faith, many Christians were appalled as people flocked into the new public church buildings, apparently taking up the cross to further their careers rather than to follow Christ.

In Egypt, groups of men and women were already moving out of the great urban centres such as Alexandria to set up radical Christian communities in the desert, determined to live out the Sermon on the Mount wholeheartedly in lives of poverty, chastity and obedience to God. Through their desire to live for God alone (in Greek the word for 'alone' is *monos*) they became known as monks.

You may have heard stories about some of the more extreme expressions of this new way of being church. One of the most extraordinary 'desert fathers' was St Simeon Stylites, who lived for 39 years on top of a tall, wide pillar, and there are plenty of other stories of men and women who went to almost incredible extremes to separate themselves from the world, out of devotion to God. We need a bit of perspective when we read stuff like this. First of all, these stories represent extremes, and no movement, including

Christianity, would want to be judged by the actions of a minority. As far as we can tell, most desert Christians did not live lives like this. The other thing to bear in mind is that the world was very different two thousand years ago, different to a degree which is almost impossible for us to comprehend as third-millennium people. The reality of the spiritual world and the life beyond this life was much more immediate than it is for most of us, and people were ready to go to great lengths to invest in this future. Many people also regarded high levels of abstinence from food, drink and sex as things to be admired, and sought after them with just as much enthusiasm as those today who believe that almost unlimited indulgence in all three is the key to a fulfilled life.

The world of the desert Christians might seem very far removed from our own, but when we read their writings and hear them speaking with their own voices, the centuries fall away and we find ourselves in touch with a spiritual wisdom which is profound, challenging and striking in its compassion. Although monastic life placed a high value on solitude and contemplation, it was lived in community where the replacement of selfishness with Christ-like sacrificial love was the ultimate goal. Within these communities, for each member there was one unique relationship – the one they had with their soul friend. Columba Stewart, in his book, *The World of the Desert Fathers*, explains what this was like:

> The fundamental human relationship in the desert was between a spiritual father and a disciple... who had come to learn the monastic way of life... Few people who came into the desert were prepared to undertake the work of monastic conversion without direction. A teacher was needed, one who could see into the heart of the novice to discover his intentions, and also through his heart **to discern the course appropriate for him**. There is also a theological truth at stake here; the elder-disciple relationship, founded upon charity, manifested **the incarnational and deeply personal nature of Christianity**.[20]

The important thing to notice here is not the formality of the teacher–learner relationship, which was of course entirely appropriate within a religious community, but rather the emphasis upon helping each individual to find their unique God-given path. What follows is even more striking:

> The abbas [spiritual fathers] in these stories… are directly involved in the struggles of their disciples while preserving the detachment necessary for true insight. They are not afraid to appear foolish or weak to make the disciple see… These abbas lead their disciples by working alongside them.

You can see immediately that this is the kind of Christianity which informed and inspired Aidan, Hilda, Cuthbert, and the other Celtic saints – walking alongside others in their struggles, willing to step down to where they are, and yet at the same time managing to keep enough distance and perspective to be able to sense what God is doing with this particular, unique person.

Given the harshness of the desert environment and the physical and spiritual toughness of the communities who lived there, the qualities which stand out so strikingly in the sayings and stories of the desert Christians are sensitivity and compassion. Here is one such story. A brother asked an old man [their term for soul friend], 'What shall I do, father, for I am not acting at all like a monk, but I eat, drink, and sleep carelessly; and I have evil thoughts and I am in great trouble, passing from one work to another and from one thought to another.' I have to say, I am immensely encouraged to learn that some of these early Christians, whose sacrificial commitment was so great compared to most of us, had exactly the same problems that we do in staying focused and not being distracted from our walk with God. I also love the simple wisdom of the soul friend's reply: the old man said, 'Sit in your cell and do the little you can untroubled.'[21]

Not surprisingly, even among people who felt they were called by God to a life of singleness, sexual temptations were a big problem.

One of the greatest contradictions of our own culture is that sex is openly depicted everywhere, and anyone who objects is regarded as ridiculously old-fashioned, and yet if anyone in a position of authority or responsibility is judged to have misbehaved sexually in any way at all, they are condemned with the utmost harshness. It is fascinating to see how the desert Christians dealt with this area.

> Another brother was attacked by lust. He got up at night, went to an old man and told him his thoughts. The old man comforted him and he returned to his cell strengthened. But the struggle began again in him. Again he went to the old man. And he did this many times. The old man did not reproach him…[22]

Once again, we are at the heart of soul friendship, knowing that we have a fellow Christian who has time for us, will listen to us without condemnation and will share our struggles. Soul friends would go to astonishing lengths with those with whom they travelled spiritually. There is another story of a monk who found the single life so difficult that he decided to leave the community and find a prostitute in a nearby town. Rather than abandon him, his soul friend went with him all the way to the pre-modern red light district, because he believed that, when confronted with the reality of his fantasies, the other man would not act on them. He was right. We might question whether such a high-risk strategy was correct, but we cannot fault the love and commitment he showed, to stay with his friend in his darkest hour.

Please do not think that the desert Christians struggled only with sexual temptations. There are accounts of many other troubles as well. I choose these examples simply because they are so different from the way that the 21st-century church often deals with this part of our human experience. One final story illustrates the kind of community which was created by such compassionate, committed and costly soul friendship. A bishop confessed before his congregation that he had had an affair. 'No longer can I be your bishop,' he told them. According to the story, the response of the congregation was to break down in tears and to say to him, 'Let this sin be upon us; only remain bishop.'[23] Presumably they had received from him the kind of soul friendship in which he listened to their struggles and failures without condemnation, and now their instinctive reaction was to offer the same to their leader in his moment of failure and weakness. 'My friends,' wrote Paul, 'if anyone is detected in a transgression, you who have received the Spirit should restore such a one in a spirit of gentleness... Bear one another's burdens, and in this way you will fulfil the law of Christ' (Galatians 6:1–2). Peter also wrote that 'love covers a multitude of sins' (1 Peter 4:8). The practice of soul friendship between individuals in the early church was an essential building block in creating the kinds of compassionate communities which were so attractive in the spread of Christian faith across Europe.

Soul Friendship in the Bible?

Some of you may be thinking that it's all very well hearing inspiring stories about remarkable Christians from long ago, but what basis is there in scripture for the practice we call soul friendship? If it is so good and so important, what does the Bible say about it?

Probably the most famous friendship in the Bible is between David and Jonathan (1 Samuel 18—20). David's remarkable tribute after Jonathan's death in battle, 'I am distressed for you, my brother Jonathan; greatly beloved were you to me; your love to me was wonderful, passing the love of women' (2 Samuel 1:26), has encouraged a lot of speculation about the precise nature of their relationship. What we know for sure is that they were both bold and courageous soldiers, both were married with children, and they seem to have seen each other as kindred spirits. Furthermore, some commentators see Jonathan's covenant with David as a recognition that the latter would become king after Jonathan's father, Saul. Seen in that light, Jonathan's voluntary resignation of his succession rights in favour of his friend is an amazingly sacrificial demonstration of the love to which David later paid tribute. Interesting as this is, however, it sheds more light on deep male friendship than on the spiritual dimension of soul friendship. For that we need to look elsewhere.

A far better example can be found earlier in the book of Samuel. For all his deep flaws as a father and a priest, Eli proved to be an excellent soul friend to the young Samuel. In 1 Samuel 3 we read how Eli helped Samuel, who 'did not yet know the Lord' (v. 7) to respond appropriately to his first encounter with God. Eli listens patiently to Samuel, discerns that God is at work, shows him how to respond to God's call and, very importantly, leaves him to engage with God himself. Whatever Eli's other failures, he helped Samuel to connect with God.

By contrast, the book of Job could be used as a textbook on how not to be a soul friend. Job's friends started well enough. When they met him after his world has been broken in pieces, 'They sat with him on the ground for seven days and seven nights, and no one spoke a word to him, for they saw that his suffering was very great' (Job 2:13). This is the right thing to do. Job needs space for grief but also to have people around him. Unfortunately, for the next 34 chapters they get it totally wrong! Each in turn tries to argue Job out of his despair, imposing their own preconceived ideas upon him and even trying to blame him for his own misfortunes. There is no real listening, no discernment, and Job is left feeling disconnected from God both personally and in the ruins of his life.

It won't be too much of a surprise to see that Jesus is the ultimate soul friend. John's Gospel is particularly interesting in this respect because the author tells fewer stories and dwells longer on each of them, often allowing longer conversations to develop. We begin with Jesus' first encounters with some of the people who will become his disciples. Again the emphasis is on allowing others space to learn and grow. Jesus offers them a welcome and an encouragement to explore. 'What are you looking for?' he asks Andrew and his friend, and 'Come and see' is his response to their interest (John 1:38–39). A few chapters further on, the encounter with the Samaritan woman at the well (4:7–30) is far more developed. With a tantalising mixture of comments, questions, observations and occasional but disarming prophetic insights, Jesus enables her to dismantle her preconceptions about God and his ways, begin to come to terms with her disordered personal history, and finally to see more clearly God's Messiah, who is, of course, the Word made flesh.

John's centrepiece miracle is the raising of Lazarus (11:1–44). One of the features of this Gospel, which is often characterised as the one that looks further into the 'spiritual' meaning of the stories of Jesus, is the amount of vivid personal detail it contains. John loves to give hints of the backstories to the events he describes. So, at the beginning of this greatest of his miracle stories, he sketches in the existing close relationship between Jesus and the family at Bethany. In speaking to Jesus, the sisters refer to Lazarus as 'he whom you love' (v. 3), and John in turn tells us that 'Jesus loved Martha and her sister and Lazarus' (v. 5). When Jesus arrives at Bethany, both sisters come to him individually, but both greet him with identical words: 'Lord, if you had been here, my brother would not have died' (vv. 21, 32).

Jesus' response is highly significant. Martha's initial words of disappointment are a prelude to her expression of uncertain but none the less real faith that Jesus can do something. Jesus gently gives shape to her belief about resurrection and draws out a deeper trust in him. Mary, by contrast, simply collapses in tears at Jesus' feet and says nothing more. Neither does Jesus, except to ask the way to the tomb. 'He was greatly disturbed in spirit and deeply moved,' John says (v. 33) – so much that, once there, 'Jesus began to weep' (v. 35). I've heard some preachers and commentators suggest that Jesus was weeping because of the unbelief of those around him, or because of the sinfulness of the world which leads to death. It was pretty obvious to the spectators, though, why Jesus was weeping: 'See how he loved him' (v. 36). It was also exactly what Mary needed. She was beyond words; she just needed someone who could come into her personal world of grief and be there too. This is the compassionate art of soul friendship, treating every single person as an individual, listening, discerning, responding appropriately and doing whatever is necessary to help them connect with God and connect God with the immediate concerns of their life.

Though not developed at such length, Jesus' sensitivity to individuals is just as visible in the other three Gospels, where he is portrayed spending far more time teaching and ministering to the crowds. In the desperate urgency of the call to go to Jairus' terminally ill daughter, Jesus still has time not only to heal but also to speak with the woman who suffered from internal bleeding (Mark 5:21–43). A more challenging but equally compassionate exchange takes place with the character we have come to know as the rich young ruler. This man approaches Jesus with an apparently genuine spiritual query: 'Good Teacher, what must I do to inherit eternal life?' (Mark 10:17). Instead of giving him a straight answer, Jesus responds with a question designed to make him think more deeply: 'Why do you call me good? No one is good but God alone' (v.18). How seriously does the man want to take his enquiry? Jesus then gives him the answer that any Jew would have given: obey the commandments. This was, after all, the way you showed that you were a faithful member of God's people. But the young man knows that Jesus has been calling into question a lot of established beliefs, so he persists in looking for a deeper answer: 'Teacher, I have kept all these since my youth' (v. 20). The response gets to the heart of what being a good soul friend is all about: 'Jesus, looking at him, loved him' (v. 21).

Jesus had many hard things to say about the rich in general, but he never lost sight of the individual in front of him. Here is a person who is at least trying to respond to God, and Jesus must be able to sense that, as well as knowing how hard it will be for him to make that response. A soul friend is also not afraid to speak the truth, no matter how challenging it may be. 'You lack one thing; go, sell what you own, and give the money to the poor, and you will have treasure in heaven; then come, follow me' (10:21). The reason why Jesus makes this seemingly outrageous demand is because 'possessions' in this context is likely to mean something much more specific than the man's general wealth. For an Israelite, the most important possession was land, seen as a gift from God, something to be defended at all costs and, of course, capable of being used to exploit economic advantages over others. All of this is at odds with the kingdom of God, which is not tied to place, nationality or ethnic background. 'When he heard this, he was shocked and went away grieving, for he had many possessions' (10:22).

We don't know what the outcome of this encounter was. We do know that Jesus did not run after him. Like a good soul friend, he clarified the challenge but knew that every person has to make their own response to God; no one can make it for them.

After Jesus, the church developed, and it is particularly interesting to see what we can learn about discipleship and pastoral care among the earliest Christians. In many respects the details are frustratingly sparse. Acts tells us that the gospel spread from Jerusalem to Rome and gives some fascinating insights into the way the message was presented to both Jews and Gentiles. It also gives us a brief snapshot of the communal life of the Jerusalem church – although there is much more we would like to know about how they learned the apostles' teaching, broke bread, shared fellowship and prayed in each other's homes (Acts 2:42). The story of Philip and the Ethiopian (8:26–40) is a masterly account of God-directed faith-sharing, but we can also see in it many of the elements of soul friendship as Philip comes alongside someone seeking after God and helps them on their spiritual journey.

The main character in Acts, however, is Saul the Pharisee, who was turned into Paul the apostle and went on to become the most prolific writer in the New Testament. We tend to think of Paul primarily as a theologian and, as a result, we tend to lose sight of the fact that all his theology was rooted in his day-to-day work as a missionary church planter and pastor of the congregations he founded. Most of

Paul's letters were written to be read aloud among gathered groups of Christians, and Luke's depiction of him in Acts largely portrays him talking to audiences, not individuals. However, one of Paul's very earliest letters, 1 Thessalonians, gives a different and very interesting perspective.

According to Acts 17:1–10, Paul and Silas only spent about three weeks in Thessalonica (during which time a number of locals came to faith) before they were forced to leave by a hostile mob. Paul's letter was therefore his only way to continue giving basic teaching to a fledgling church. This is a very personal letter as Paul recalls his first meetings with the Thessalonians:

> As you know and as God is our witness, we never came with words of flattery or with a pretext for greed; nor did we seek praise from mortals, whether from you or from others, though we might have made demands as apostles of Christ. But we were gentle among you, like a nurse tenderly caring for her own children. So deeply do we care for you that we are determined to share with you not only the gospel of God but also our own selves, because you have become very dear to us.
> 1 THESSALONIANS 2:5–8

Clearly, in that short space of time, Paul and Silas came to know this group of people very well indeed. Paul goes on to describe how he helped them to get established in the Christian faith.

> You remember our labour and toil, brothers and sisters; we worked night and day, so that we might not burden any of you while we proclaimed to you the gospel of God. You are witnesses, and God also, how pure, upright, and blameless our conduct was towards you believers. As you know, we dealt with each one of you like a father with his children, urging and encouraging you and pleading that you should lead a life worthy of God, who calls you into his own kingdom and glory.
> 1 THESSALONIANS 2:9–12

As in all his letters to churches, when Paul refers to 'you' he means a group of people, but here he writes specifically of how he and Silas 'dealt with each one of you'. Their ministry was to individuals, not just to a group. Paul's images are also striking. In the previous passage he was like a nurse caring for children, and in this one like a father. Both images speak of personal, individual care for the well-being of the Thessalonian Christians.

Summing up, none of these passages give a template for what later Christians called 'soul friendship', but they do show how Jesus, Paul and the early church ministered to the spiritual needs of individuals. It seems that, in addition to the three dimensions of Christian pastoral care and discipleship – teaching (for example, Acts 20:7), meeting in groups (2:46) and crisis pastoral interventions (the letter to Philemon) – there was a fourth dimension of coming alongside individuals to help in their discipleship and spiritual growth. Soul friendship gives a practical model for rediscovering this neglected fourth dimension.

Soul friendship today

The value of one-to-one support and encouragement is being rediscovered everywhere today. Mentoring is common in the workplace and in education to help employees or students to realise their full potential, particularly in the early stages of a new job or course. 'Life coaching' has become very popular in recent years as a way of helping people to move towards their goals in a broad range of life situations, not least by examining the attitudes and behaviours which may hinder them. Within Christianity, there has simultaneously been a reawakening of interest in the art of 'spiritual direction', a practice often associated with the more Catholic wing of the church but being adopted in varying forms across the traditions.

I have recently given up trying to define the difference between spiritual direction and soul friendship. Penny Warren, one of the other Guardians or leaders of the Community of Aidan and Hilda, was recently a delegate at the Spiritual Directors of Europe Conference. Having met people from 16 different nationalities, she reported to us that there really is no difference between what some people call spiritual direction and what we call soul friendship. That's good enough for me!

That said, I do think the terminology matters a bit. For some people, the term spiritual *director* sounds very authoritarian, as if someone is going to give us orders about our walk with God and put us right if we stray. The truth is, as all good spiritual directors will be quick to point out, the only true director is the Holy Spirit, and they are just trying to help 'directees' to discern more clearly what God is doing and respond appropriately. The other problem – though this is both a strength and a weakness, depending on how you look at it – is that spiritual direction tends to be seen as a highly specialised ministry requiring lengthy and often quite expensive training. As a result, only a relatively small number of Christians get involved in it.

There's absolutely nothing wrong with people being experts: far from it. If someone starts poking around under the bonnet of my car, I definitely want them to know what they're doing. In the same way, if I give someone access to the inside of my relationship with God, I want them to know what they are doing. That said, if it is beneficial for all of us to have someone with whom we can share our journey with God, there simply will not be enough experts to go round. As with most areas of ministry in the church, I think it is likely that we will see some people who are more gifted than others, with the motivation and ability to train at a far more expert level. Equally, I think we ought to expect to see plenty of ordinary Christians being used by God to get alongside others and encourage them on their journey. For both these reasons, therefore, I prefer to use the term 'soul friend' rather than 'spiritual director'.

Whenever I say this publically, I nearly always get a queue of indignant spiritual directors coming to tell me that I have misunderstood them. Before I go any further, let me say that if you are a trained spiritual director, you are one of the most valuable people in the church today, and that without your gifts, skills and expertise, it would not be possible to do any of the things I am outlining here. Equally, if you're fortunate enough to know someone who is a trained spiritual director, I hope that one consequence of reading this book is that you will go and make use of their gifts, if you're not doing so already. So, hoping that we won't fall out, let's see what modern soul friendship might look like in practice in the kind of Christian community setting I'm describing. Let's start with a definition.

> A Soul Friend is a mature Christian who is in sympathy with our Way of Life, and who helps us to discern and respond appropriately to God's will, grow in maturity, responsibility and wholeness, and to deepen our relationship with God.

Our Soul Friend also helps us initially to work out our personal application of the Way of Life, reviews it with us at regular intervals, and is a companion to us on our spiritual journey. How often you meet with your Soul Friend is a matter of personal preference. Twice a year is probably the minimum in order to keep any sense of continuity, and three times a year works well for a lot of people. Currently, most of the people I meet with prefer a two-monthly pattern and we normally meet for about an hour or an hour and a half.

So what happens? In essence, a Soul Friend does four things:

- Listening as the other person shares what has happened in their journey with God since the last meeting.
- Helping the other person discern what God is doing in their life at this time and how they might respond.
- Discussing with the other person their personal application of the Way of Life.
- Praying with the other person.

This may sound rather like what happens in a prayer partnership or one of the many similar and useful ways congregations have developed to encourage their members to meet during the week. There is one essential difference, however. When a person meets with their Soul Friend, it is vital that the Soul Friend gives their full and undivided attention to the other person, in order to listen to them and help them make greater sense of what God is currently doing in their life. This is not a time for *mutual* sharing and support. The great value of spending time with your Soul Friend is that they are there exclusively for you. In a meeting such as a prayer partnership, where two people will share needs with one another, it is all too easy for each to be aware of their own needs and desire to talk while they are meant to be listening to the other. Anyone who is a Soul Friend to others will have a Soul Friend of their own with whom they will discuss their own journey with God. This enables them to be free to give their full attention to the one coming to them, without the intrusion of their own needs and agendas.

For this reason it is generally better that two people are not Soul Friends to one another, since the boundaries necessary for such a relationship to work properly can easily become blurred. That said, it is not impossible, and we know that some of the great desert Christians were Soul Friends to each other. Nevertheless, where such partnerships do exist, it is essential when they meet that one person remains in the Soul Friend role throughout in order to give their full attention to the other, and it is almost certainly best for them to arrange to meet on a separate occasion to swap roles. Needless to say, Soul Friendship is not meant to replace other types of church gatherings, and those involved may still be part of a prayer partnership, home group, task group or any other type of gathering. It is just important to stress that meeting for the purposes of Soul Friendship is something different.

Over time, people will develop a high degree of transparency with their Soul Friend because they will find that this relationship of trust and encouragement makes it possible for them to talk about things which they might never feel confident to reveal elsewhere. It should therefore go without saying that a Soul Friend must be able to maintain absolute confidentiality. This can, however, seem like a potentially burdensome or even worrying level of responsibility. It is vital to be aware that *in extreme cases there are exceptions to absolute confidentiality, where it can, and indeed should, be broken.* Such instances would be where someone is involved in actions which are illegal, harmful or abusive to others, or where there is a potential for self-harm. In those circumstances it would be right to disclose information about the situation to an appropriate person who is qualified to deal with it. Such a situation is extremely unlikely but it is important for people getting involved in Soul Friendship to know that they are protected so that their ministry remains a joy and not a burden.

There may, of course, be other circumstances in which a Soul Friend may wish to seek confidential advice from their own Soul Friend, their minister or someone else whose knowledge and experience goes beyond their own: perhaps the person they are meeting has shared a need for growth, help or guidance which exceeds what they themselves can offer. People may seek counsel from their Soul Friend, but Soul Friendship is not a form of counselling. In very broad terms, counselling is about solving personal and spiritual problems, whereas Soul Friendship is as much opportunity-centred as it is problem-centred. If a person needs counselling for a particular issue, it is best to point them towards specialist help. Equally, a person might talk about their desire to grow and develop in a particular area of their life or to gain skills which will complement their God-given gifts. Again, the role of the Soul Friend is not to have all the answers but rather to help the person find the teacher or course that will equip them. Keep in mind at all times that the role of the Soul Friend is to help the other person to discern what God is doing in their life at the present time and to respond in an appropriate way.

What kind of person makes an effective Soul Friend? Do you have to be a fictional super-Christian like Jon Darrow? Is it the kind of role where perhaps only Jesus would meet the job spec? It sounds like a huge ask, but I believe that, as in many areas of Christian life, a great many of us can make a useful contribution if we're prepared to offer God what we've got and be willing to learn and grow in our areas of ignorance or inexperience.

In his book *A Guide for Soul Friends*, Ray Simpson, the Founding Guardian of the Community of Aidan and Hilda, sets out a model of Soul Friendship which allows beginners to get involved and then progress to higher levels of skill and ability. He suggests four qualities that need to be cultivated by those who want to offer Soul Friendship to others:

- Foster the habit of daily reflection.
- Walk closely with God.
- Spend time in prayer.
- Develop listening skills.[24]

I prefer to look at these qualities in a different order.

1 Develop listening skills

There are plenty of mature Christians able to teach and encourage others, but essential to the role of the Soul Friend is the ability to listen, both to the other person and to God. Many of us, perhaps especially those of us who are involved in any kind of recognised Christian ministry, have a well-intentioned desire to fix other people! Too often we find ourselves telling people answers before they have even finished their question, which can mean we end up responding to what we expect them to say, not what they are actually saying. Likewise, some of us respond to other people's stories by immediately sharing a similar experience of our own. 'Oh yes, I've had that. Horrible isn't it?' or 'Do you know, something very similar happened to me and…'. While this sounds sympathetic, we are actually shifting the focus on to our own experience rather than that of the person speaking. We can also assume that we know what

God's will is for a particular situation before we've even asked God. As a late friend of mine used to say, 'assumption is the mother of all mess-ups'. (Actually he used a less polite expression!) The ability to listen instead of talking is essential for a Soul Friend and, for most of us, it has to be cultivated.

2 Foster the habit of daily reflection

Not only do we need to listen to others and to God, but we also need to think about what we hear, and we cannot help others to do that if we are not doing it ourselves.

Many Christians today are discovering a form of prayer called the daily examen, which has been described as a technique of prayerful reflection on the events of the day in order to detect God's presence and discern his direction for us. Its origins are in Ignatian spirituality, the approach to Christian life developed by the 16th-century saint, Ignatius Loyola. Here is a simple way to go about it.

- Become aware of God's presence. Look back on the events of the day in the company of the Holy Spirit. The day may seem confusing to you – a blur, a jumble, a muddle. Ask God to bring clarity and understanding.
- Review the day with gratitude. Gratitude is the foundation of our relationship with God. Walk through your day in the presence of God and note its joys and delights. Focus on the day's gifts. Look at the work you did, the people you interacted with. What did you receive from these people? What did you give them? Pay attention to small things – the food you ate, the sights you saw, and other seemingly small pleasures. God is in the details.
- Pay attention to your emotions. One of St Ignatius's great insights was that we detect the presence of the Spirit of God in the movements of our emotions. Reflect on the feelings you experienced during the day. Boredom? Elation? Resentment? Compassion? Anger? Confidence? What is God saying through these feelings?

- Choose one feature of the day and pray from it. Ask the Holy Spirit to direct you to something during the day that God thinks is particularly important. It may involve a feeling, positive or negative. It may be a significant encounter with another person or a vivid moment of pleasure or peace, or it may be something that seems rather insignificant. Look at it. Pray about it. Allow the prayer to arise spontaneously from your heart – whether intercession, praise, repentance or gratitude.
- Look toward tomorrow. Ask God to give you light for tomorrow's challenges. Pay attention to the feelings that surface as you survey what's coming up. Are you doubtful? Cheerful? Apprehensive? Full of delighted anticipation? Allow these feelings to turn into prayer. Seek God's guidance. Ask him for help and understanding. Pray for hope.[25]

For those of us who are too tired to concentrate this hard at the end of the day, I quite like a simpler form in the Community of Aidan and Hilda's Night Prayer, which simply says, 'May that part of me that did not grow at morning grow at nightfall.' It normally only takes a few moments to see what we could thank God for in the last 24 hours, and what could have gone better, and to turn them into prayer, Learning to be reflective really is as simple as that, but it needs to be established as a regular practice in our lives in order to become truly embedded.

3 Spend time in prayer

No surprises here! At the same time, this is an area in which many Christians quickly generate a high level of guilt because none of us will say that our prayer life is all that we would want it to be. The point is not that we are spending hours in prayer each day but rather that we have a personal pattern of prayer which expresses a genuine connection with God. The fact that this is sometimes a struggle, and that we are constantly in a process of learning and relearning, is a qualification, not a hindrance, to being a Soul Friend to others. In Jesus himself, 'we do not have a high priest who is unable to sympathise with our weaknesses, but we have one who in every respect has been tested as we are' (Hebrews 4:15), and a good Soul Friend also needs to know what it is like to struggle. Prayerful reflection on our own experience may give us insights into how to pray for others.

4 Walk closely with God

OK, how do you define this? I'm not even sure I'm going to try, except to say that most of us know a close walk with God when we see it. The whole argument of this book is that, to create lasting community, we need to become people who are intentional about our relationship with God, people who know that they are on a journey and not just drifting. Walking closely with God starts from wanting to walk closely with God, and then beginning to do things which will make that closeness more of a reality. It does not mean that we will always succeed or that we will spend every day dazzled by a glorious sense of God's immediate presence. One of the first things I was taught when I became a Christian as a teenager was to 'keep short accounts with God'. People who walk closely with God are quick to recognise their own faults, quick to bring them to God and quick to remember that his forgiveness is freely given again and again and again. People who walk closely with God are not people who never fall over, but they are people who get back up again and walk on.

If you recognise the importance of these four qualities for your own life, and are making a beginning, however falteringly, to cultivate them, you have the qualities which God could use to make you a Soul Friend to someone else. In the last chapter of this book I will say more about how you can begin to travel down this road, but it is now time to look at the third element in creating community, one in which all Soul Friends will need to be rooted – joining in a rhythm of prayer.

Chapter 4

Joining in a rhythm of prayer

What can you say about prayer which hasn't been said a million times already? Last year I taught a course on Celtic spirituality for people from other churches in our area. Along the way, as we looked at the deep prayer life of the first-millennium Celtic Christian communities, I asked people how their churches encouraged them in their individual praying and how it gave them opportunities to pray together. There was a long silence. 'I don't know,' was the first answer. 'Fails miserably,' was the second. Finally it emerged that some of the churches did teach courses on prayer and that one or two held services of Morning or Evening Prayer, even if hardly anyone knew about them. But the initial response was, to say the least, worrying. In our different churches we don't seem to be teaching and modelling good ways of praying, nearly as much as we should – so perhaps there is a need to say something fresh about prayer.

On top of that, there seems to be no shortage of Christians who feel anywhere between vaguely unhappy and utterly depressed about their praying. One of the reasons I've come to value the practice of Soul Friendship so highly is that it gives me an opportunity to find out how people pray and how they feel about it – and, more often than not, an opportunity to tell them that they are actually doing much better than they thought they were. Prayer really ought to be a lot easier than many people seem to find it.

Here's another reason why there might be something more to say about prayer. Depending on which stream of Christianity you identify with, you will probably want to pray in a way that you believe to be 'biblical' or that you see as being in tune with the historic traditions of the church. When I started to look more deeply into the prayer lives of the early Christian communities, I discovered that some of my basic assumptions about how to pray, going right back to when I became a Christian as a teenager and began to pray meaningfully, were diametrically opposite to some of the assumptions held by Jesus and the early Christians. This did not mean that the way I and many other Christians were praying was wrong, simply that there was a whole dimension to prayer and an attitude to prayer which we seemed to have missed.

A journey of prayer

It feels incredibly presumptuous to be writing about prayer. If you are anything like me, you may have one of two reactions if you read a book on prayer. Either you will have the uneasy feeling that the author seems to see many more answers to prayer, a lot more often, than you do, or you will have the equally uneasy feeling that the author floats through life on a cushion of deep peace created by their hours of contemplation. That is a bit of an exaggeration, but I want you to know that I write about prayer as someone for whom prayer is often a daily battle, but who knows deep down that it is a battle absolutely worth fighting. It's therefore worth telling you a bit about my own journey of discovery as far as prayer is concerned.

Church was not part of my life when I was growing up. Somewhere along the way, I learned to recite the Lord's Prayer, but it was no more than that – just saying words from time to time. I'm not even sure I understood them, let alone had a sense that God would respond in any way. All of that changed when I became a Christian. The first thing I was taught was that it was vital to pray and read the Bible every day. This was something personal and individual, although I was given Scripture Union Bible reading notes to help me make sense of it all. The second thing I learned was that Christians were supposed to pray together, and this involved sitting in a group and taking turns to pray out loud.

Now, even as you read these words, I know that some of you are already feeling a rising sense of trauma and anxiety. A surprising number of Christians would rather swim in a pool of piranhas than pray out loud in front of anyone else. Although personality plays its part – some of us are introverts rather than extraverts – I think a lot of this is to do with expectations. Talking to Christians from more traditional church backgrounds, I have discovered that 'reverence', 'devotion' and 'holiness' are associated in their minds with being very quiet, so speaking aloud in prayer (except in a liturgy) simply goes against the grain. I am so glad I encountered praying aloud right at the beginning of my Christian experience, and that it was regarded as completely normal and not a big deal. Consequently I never had any inhibitions about it. Check the psalms and you will also find that people who were holy and devoted, revering God with all their heart, were capable of being very vocal and expressive as they were doing it. I should also say that I appreciate how difficult this is for many Christians but, if you read on, you may find some insights to help you feel more at ease.

So I knew what I was supposed to do, even if doing it was sometimes another thing entirely. A big boost came through encountering charismatic renewal when I was 18. Upgrading the presence and power of the Holy Spirit from an idea to an experience gave prayer an energy, spontaneity and reality which had previously been lacking. Going to university was one of the best things that ever happened to my life as a Christian. Initially I found only one other person who was an active Christian. This meant that nearly all of my friends were not Christians, and a surprising number of them were interested in asking what real Christianity was all about, so that over time a number of them came to faith themselves.

The university Christian Union was focused on evangelism, which made it easy to get involved as I had lots of non-Christian friends asking me about my faith anyway. The group also understood that prayer was essential if mission was going to be effective. Every Saturday about 100 students would gather in a hall at lunchtime for an hour of prayer. The focus and intensity of it stays with me even today – big rugby players reading aloud passages of psalms in praise to God, and reserved academic high flyers interceding for the persecuted church behind the then Iron Curtain. I remember also the run-up to a big university mission as we gathered in a chapel for a special prayer meeting. There were far too few seats in the pews so people sat on the floor along the walls in the subdued light, with the painted faces of academics from previous centuries looking down on us. At one point we were asked simply to name aloud all our friends who we hoped would come to faith. For the next few minutes an unbroken litany of names rose in a growing murmur of voices on every side. There was a profound sense of the all-embracing compassion of the God to whom every single person matters, as well as a deep sense of being united in something that mattered.

I think it was Archbishop William Temple who said, 'When I pray, coincidences happen. When I don't pray, they don't happen.' During the big mission week, we were trying to invite all our friends to hear the guest speaker. There had been plenty of late-night conversations round bottles of wine and whisky, so this was not exactly cold calling for me, but I was a bit surprised by one friend who reacted to a friendly invitation by screaming 'No!' and promptly running away upstairs to slam her door. 'OK,' I thought. 'Not sure what's going on there.' So off we went without her – or so I thought. Later that night, I found out that she had gone on her own to hear the talk, and had been so impressed by what she heard that she decided to commit herself as a Christian on the spot. When I met up with her a few years on, she was helping to lead the youth group in a church in Brussels. When we pray, coincidences happen. When we don't pray, they don't seem to happen.

There is a danger, however, that most of our praying becomes like battering God with a series of requests, even if they are for good things. The other side of prayer is listening, and this again is an area that many people find hard. It used to drive me mad listening to talks in churches where the speaker or service leader would say,

'Now let's spend a few minutes waiting on the Lord and allowing him to speak to us.' I wanted to get up and yell, 'Great – but how do you do it?' The charismatic renewal movement has done a vital job in helping the church regain an awareness of the gift of prophecy, cultivating openness to the different ways that God can impress his thoughts upon us and so speak to us. The other way in is through the rediscovery of various ways of meditative or contemplative prayer, which seek to cultivate an inner stillness that makes us more receptive to God's thoughts.

One more personal story will serve to illustrate just how important prayer is in the life of the local church. For 14 years we wrestled with the problem of our second church building, a beautiful 17th-century chapel with a structurally unsound 20th-century extension which made itredundant in 1995. The congregation battled on in the church hall next to a huge crumbling mass of brick and concrete, which was too expensive to demolish but declared to the world, 'We are closed' for the whole time it stood empty. The only way to fund the restoration was by selling the church hall, and in 2003 we thought we had found the ideal buyer – a Health Service clinic, quietly and unobtrusively treating people with various addictions. The local community thought otherwise. Fuelled by lurid images of stoned drug addicts slumped in their doorways, in no time at all they had got 400 frightened signatures on a petition calling on us to abandon the sale. We were caught in an awful dilemma. The professional advice we were given told us we had no option but to sell to the highest bidder, which was the clinic, yet if we did so we would earn the undying opposition of many of the local people we wanted to reach and serve.

In the middle of it all, the trainee minister on placement with us told me that she had seen a clear picture in her mind as she was praying. 'I had a vision of a strong oak door that was slightly open. It was being pushed shut on one side, but on the other side I could see a very bright light and a small old church. I also heard a voice saying, "My vision will not be closed. The people on the outside will come to understand my plans."' This picture was not from someone who normally goes around saying, 'The Lord told me…' so it needed to be taken seriously – and besides, the human advice we were getting was not much help! Should we push ahead and hope the local people would come round? That seemed unlikely. Then another possibility opened up. This could be a door of opportunity to connect seriously with a neighbourhood who thought we were dead and gone, and maybe it was the property experts whose advice was pushing this door shut. We decided to go against the professional guidance and abort the sale, trusting that somehow God would show us another way of financing the project into which we believed he had led us. The local reaction was simply amazing. The *Ealing Gazette* ran a story saying that we were the church who listened to local people. We got a warm round of applause when we reported back to the local residents' meeting, and, although the story still had plenty of twists and turns, in 2010 we reopened the restored church of St Mary, West Twyford. Is it any wonder that Paul told the Corinthians to 'strive for the spiritual gifts, and especially that you may prophesy' (1 Corinthians 14:1). One of the psalms of Asaph pleads, 'O that my people would listen…' (Psalm 81:13).

I may be giving the impression that I have had a lot of good experiences of prayer – and I have – but it has not been, and is still not, always easy to pray even with all these encouragements. This particular struggle is the final piece of the jigsaw in seeing how a rhythm of prayer is essential to creating both Christian community and a healthy connection between God and the whole of life.

You might think that being in full-time paid Christian ministry is one of the biggest boosts anyone could have to their prayer life. After all, prayer is an essential part of the job, so there must be plenty of time, opportunity and motivation to pray. Sadly, it's not always quite like that. We live in a frantically busy world, and the church is often no different. There are enough meetings, phone calls, emails, paperwork, people to see and things to do to keep ministers busy from morning till night, six days a week, and even then the 'To do' list never seems to get any shorter. Shortly after being ordained, I found that my established habit of prayer and Bible reading at the start of each day was getting more and more squeezed, especially if I was feeling tired and struggling to concentrate. More worrying was the sense, at the end of too many evenings, that I had checked in with God in the morning and then passed the rest of the day with very little acknowledgment of his presence. This clearly was not healthy and I started to wonder what was missing.

Everything I had ever learned about prayer emphasised that it should be personal, spontaneous and from the heart. Hadn't Jesus warned against 'vain repetition' in the Sermon on the Mount? And yet that spontaneity did not reflect the way many Christians, down many centuries, had actually prayed. We had a rich tradition of written prayers and time-tested patterns of praying which had sustained millions of believers in a living relationship with God. Using the patterns developed by the part of the church to which I belong, I began to use the written forms of Morning and sometimes Evening Prayer, and discovered something in them which I never expected – freedom and life. I learned that there is nothing wrong with praying in someone else's words, if they say what you want to say as well as or better than you could say it. I learned that, over time, prayerfully reading the Psalms day by day immerses you in a wider and deeper language of prayer than most of us will develop on our own. I also learned that, on the days when you know deep down that you need to pray but you feel too tired, or your mind is so overloaded that concentration flies away like a sweet paper in the wind, simply reading someone else's words is still valid prayer. The structure of these daily forms of prayer, known traditionally as Offices, gives us a firm foundation from which to launch our own personal prayer, and fertile soil in which it can grow.

Rediscovering roots and rhythms

Without realising it at the time, in discovering for myself these time-honoured and life-giving patterns of prayer, I had also stumbled upon something truly ancient, going right back to Jesus and beyond, a way of praying which the Bible simply takes for granted.

Because Jesus was so often in conflict with the Pharisees, a group of people who chose to practise their Jewish faith with fanatical zeal, we sometimes assume that he was simply sweeping away most of the religious practices of his people. 'You have heard that it was said… but I say to you…' runs through the Sermon on the Mount like a refrain, and it sounds as if Jesus had no time for older ways of doing things. Here's a question: how many times do you think Jesus went up to the Passover in Jerusalem? Because Matthew, Mark and Luke only describe the Passover in the week when Jesus died, a lot of Christians get the impression that he went only once. John, however, describes several different occasions. In fact, it's highly likely that, like hundreds of thousands of other Jews, Jesus made the pilgrimage to Jerusalem nearly every year. Judaism, the faith of the Old Testament which is foundational to our own faith, punctuates the year with festivals designed to help people remember and connect with God. In between these special times, there was weekly worship in the synagogue, and between sabbaths, practised by the majority of Jews including Jesus and the disciples, was a pattern of daily prayer.

According to Deuteronomy, Moses had given the Israelites clear teaching on how they were to honour and remember God when they entered the land he was giving them:

Hear, O Israel: The Lord is our God, the Lord alone. You shall love the Lord your God with all your heart, and with all your soul, and with all your might. Keep these words that I am commanding you today in your heart. **Recite them** to your children and talk about them when you are at home and when you are away, **when you lie down and when you rise.** Bind them as a sign on your hand, fix them as an emblem on your forehead, and write them on the doorposts of your house and on your gates.

DEUTERONOMY 6:4–9, emphasis added

This command became known, from its opening Hebrew word, as the Shema, and it became the defining Jewish creed and prayer, to be said at the beginning and end of the day. Nowhere does the Old Testament command daily prayer, but this was how the overwhelming majority of Jews would have interpreted these words. The first-century Jewish historian Josephus, one of our best sources for the New Testament period, speaks about this passage and understands it to mean not only that Moses commanded the Shema to be recited but that it should be accompanied, morning and evening, by prayers of thanksgiving.[26] Furthermore, the commandment in Deuteronomy makes it clear that this recitation should take place not in the temple or the synagogue but at home or away from home – in fact, wherever a devoted Jew happened to be. These daily prayers are echoed in the psalms: 'It is good to give thanks to the Lord, to sing praises to your name, O Most High; to declare your steadfast love in the morning, and your faithfulness by night' (Psalm 92:1–2).

For more devoted Jews, stopping deliberately to pray twice a day was not enough. We read that Daniel got into trouble when he defied a command to pray only to King Darius: instead 'he continued to go to his house, which had windows in its upper room open towards Jerusalem, and to get down on his knees three times a day to pray to his God and praise him, just as he had done previously' (Daniel 6:10). For some very devoted Jews, even this was not enough. The author of Psalm 119 mentions in passing, 'Seven times day I praise you for your righteous ordinances' (v. 164).

Bearing in mind these prayer practices, common to all Jews, jump forward to the New Testament. We know that prayer was of central importance to Jesus, and that through it he communed regularly and intimately with God as his Father in a way which caused his disciples to ask him for advice on how to pray (Luke 11:1). What we easily miss, however, is the regular structure and pattern of prayer which Jesus observed anyway, like any other Jew. Take two passages which are often used to illustrate the intensity of Jesus' prayer life. 'In the morning, while it was still very dark, he got up and went out to a deserted place, and there he prayed' (Mark 1:35). 'After he had dismissed the crowds, he went up the mountain by himself to pray. When evening came, he was there alone' (Matthew 14:23). The amount of time Jesus devoted to prayer is remarkable, especially when we realise how tired he would have been on both occasions after long periods of involvement with the crowds. His desire for solitude is also notable, but what frequently gets overlooked is not how long Jesus prayed, or with whom, but when he prayed: morning and evening. The intimacy and spontaneity of Jesus' prayer life were carried by the time-honoured structures of prayer which he learned from his people and could be traced back deep into their scriptures.

We know frustratingly little about the worship and prayer practices of the New Testament church, and we are sorely tempted simply to read back into it whatever is familiar to us. Nevertheless, there are tantalising hints. Many scholars think that Luke's portrait of the Jerusalem church may be somewhat idealised, but even if it is, it still tells us what the early Christians thought the ideal should be. After Pentecost, the new Christians 'devoted themselves to the apostles' teaching and fellowship, to the breaking of bread and the prayers' (Acts 2:42). Notice that it says 'the prayers', not just prayer in general. This suggests that, as often as possible, the first Christian church made it a priority to take part in the daily worship in the temple. There were, of course, no church buildings and for several centuries Christians met together in homes. It therefore comes as no surprise to read on that 'day by day, as they spent much time together in the temple, they broke bread at home... praising God' (vv. 46–47). It's hard to escape the conclusion that, no doubt with renewed vitality and spontaneity, the first Christians carried on praying daily in families or groups, just like other Jews. We see this confirmed by Peter and John 'going up to the temple at the hour of prayer, at three o'clock in the afternoon' (3:1), and also by Peter's vision before the conversion of Cornelius the Gentile centurion, which occurred 'about noon... as... Peter went up on the roof to pray' (10:9). This is exactly the time when a devout Jew like Peter would be having his second daily prayer time.

We know a great deal about Paul's prayers because in his letters he often tells people exactly what he has been praying for them. Unfortunately we know almost nothing about his own pattern of prayer or what he taught in the churches he founded. A little detective work may give us some clues, however. Paul tells us that he adapted his approach according to whether he was among Jews or non-Jews (1 Corinthians 9:19–23). This meant thorough observance of the Jewish law – presumably not too hard for an ex-Pharisee – when working among Jewish people. Acts confirms this picture, as we see Paul frequently going first to the local synagogue on his missionary journeys. Yet, however strongly Paul insisted that Jewish laws and customs must not be imposed upon non-Jewish converts, it seems that his own Jewish practices stayed with him. Luke tells us that on one occasion he followed the Jewish custom of making and performing a personal vow to God (Acts 18:18) and that when he returned to Jerusalem for the last time, he was eager to get there in time to celebrate the Jewish festival of Pentecost (20:16). These little hints suggest that the famous apostle to the Gentiles stayed true to his Jewish roots in his personal walk with God. Stopping for daily prayer two or three times a day would have been an integral part of that spirituality.

From there it might be possible to suggest that when Paul says he prayed 'night and day' to see the Thessalonians again (1 Thessalonians 3:10), he was not just speaking figuratively or with emphasis, but referring to the fact that when he prayed at the beginning and end of each day, he prayed for them. Going further, Paul reminds the Corinthians that 'in Christ Jesus I became your father through the gospel. I appeal to you, then, be imitators of me' (1 Corinthians 4:15–16), and he praises the Thessalonians for imitating him so well and becoming an example to others (1 Thessalonians 1:6–7). If encouraging personal imitation was Paul's standard way of teaching, then we might reasonably guess that the prayer patterns of the early churches round the Mediterranean were modelled on the Jewish practices of prayer which Paul himself probably followed – a daily rhythm of turning aside to God.

If we need some careful detective work and perhaps a little inspired guesswork to get a picture of how the New Testament church prayed, everything emerges much more clearly, like mist burning off the hills, a couple of centuries later. What emerges is not only striking but also surprising and challenging for many of our inherited understandings of prayer. The *Didache*, a collection of teachings dated somewhere between the end of the first century and the mid-second century, urges Christians to pray the Lord's Prayer three times a day, and this looks remarkably like a continuation of the Jewish prayer rhythms we have seen already. Over the next two centuries, many of the great writers and teachers whom we refer to as the Early Church Fathers, such as Tertullian, Cyprian, Origen and Clement of Alexandria, all encourage daily patterns of prayer designed to help ordinary Christians to obey Paul's instruction to 'pray without ceasing' (1 Thessalonians 5:17). Most of this prayer would have gone on in homes or wherever a handful of Christians might gather, not least because, until Christianity became the official religion of the Roman Empire in the fourth century, it had no public buildings.

The early Christians' understanding of what they were doing when they prayed is striking. Cyprian, the great third-century bishop and martyr, wrote:

> The Teacher of peace and Master of unity would not have prayer be made singly and individually, so that when one prays, he does not pray for himself alone... Our prayer is public and common; and when we pray, we pray not for one, but for the whole people, because we the whole people are one.[27]

In other words, even when Christians were praying on their own, they were conscious that they were praying with the rest of the Christian community – an awareness helped, no doubt, by the fact that they were often praying at a similar time of day to other believers. A century later, these underground streams that we have traced from their sources in the Old Testament, through bubbling springs in the New Testament and clearer channels in the early church period, burst to the surface as Christianity was finally able to go public. In the major cities of the empire, churches were built. They offered morning and evening prayer services and, by all contemporary accounts, they were packed to the doors.

This leads to an extraordinary conclusion, which goes against almost everything that we as modern Western Christians have been taught. We think of prayer first and foremost as something private and personal, which goes on between me and God. After all, didn't Jesus rebuke the Pharisees for praying in public, and tell us to pray to our Father in secret (Matthew 6:5–6)? What many of us won't realise was that the private room to which Jesus was referring was, in most houses, the store cupboard. He was concerned not with the location in which people were to pray, but the attitude with which they prayed. Were they doing it for an audience of one, namely God, or in order to impress other people in a society that took prayer seriously? It's quite obvious from Jesus' other comments about prayer (for example, 'When two or three are gathered in my name...', Matthew 18:20), and from everything we have uncovered about how he and other Jews prayed, that he was not saying the only valid way to pray was individually and in private. Instead, all the evidence points in precisely the other direction. Whereas we think of prayer as private first and something we do with others second, *the early Christians thought of prayer primarily as something we do with others, and of prayer on our own as being an extension of it.*

Thus the gigantic link is made between prayer and community. When the first Christians prayed they were not just expressing their connection with God but also their connection with each other. Even when they were on their own, their patterns of prayer still reinforced their understanding that they were praying not only for but also with their fellow Christians.

The early monastic communities took this insight even further. They were inspired, indeed captivated, by Paul's command to pray without ceasing. Their vocation and passion were to find ways in which they could consciously connect God with every part of life. For them, the regular prayer times throughout the day and night, increasing to as many as seven in number, were ways in which they maintained their focus that everything they did was being done with and for God, a focus which they took with them back into their periods of work or study. Even though many of them spent extended periods in solitude, they would come together in order to pray, carrying with them the words of the psalms which were at the heart of their worship, to meditate upon them while they were engaged again in manual labour. Prayer and community were deeply linked.

Contemporary 'new monastic' communities such as the Community of Aidan and Hilda, the Northumbria Community and many others have rediscovered the immense value of daily prayer rhythms and are exploring creative ways of making them work amid the busyness and complexity of 21st-century life. Even though we are dispersed communities, we have learned that following these rhythms of prayer not only keeps alive our connection with God, but also helps us to stay connected with one another.

Whenever I spend a few days on the Holy Island of Lindisfarne, I always feel as though the metronome of my prayer life is being recalibrated and restored to a regular rhythm. Life on the island begins with Morning Prayer in the parish church at 7.30am, and this happens all year round. I remember the first time I went there, in late October 2000. Clouds were racing across the sky, driven by a bracing wind, as I walked through the village and saw the remains of the medieval priory silhouetted against the red dawn. It struck me, as the next gust blasted in, that while Celtic Christianity was inspiring, those early monks must have been tough, and there wasn't much room for sentimentality. People gather in the church again at 5.30pm for Evening Prayer. In between, the Community of Aidan and Hilda's retreat house, the Open Gate, holds midday prayer in its atmospheric basement chapel and winds the day to its conclusion with Night Prayer. Even when we are on the island for Community Council meetings, cramming as much work as possible into 24 hours together as we gather from the corners of the UK, we still make time to observe these rhythms of prayer, and it does make a difference.

Another vital aspect of the rhythm of prayer is praying for one another. The Community has a daily prayer diary, covering all of its members. As I write this, I have just come back from a trip to the winding lanes of rural Devon, where Penny Warren, already mentioned as one of the three Guardians of the Community, was making her promises to become a life member. There was a congregation of about 30 people in the ancient country church, but Penny will have been aware, as I was, that 300 people across five continents were praying for her that day. This is community. Ray Simpson, our founding Guardian, started working a lot of this stuff out in practice in a remarkable interdenominational church at Bowthorpe in East Anglia. They established a pattern of meeting together, as many people as possible, for daily prayer. Ray comments that if he ever wanted to know what was going on in the church, and where the pastoral needs were, he simply had to turn up to daily prayer and listen to what people were praying about.

Planting new patterns of prayer

When Thomas Cranmer started writing the Book of Common Prayer for the newly founded Church of England in the 16th century, he was determined to get rid of the elements that he and others regarded as unnecessary junk, which had obscured true Christian worship in the late Middle Ages. Lots of things disappeared. Other parts were radically redesigned, but one thing that Cranmer kept was the structure of Morning and Evening Prayer, subtitled 'daily throughout the year'. It was a great vision: people would go to their work in the morning, stopping to meet with God, and return at the end of the working day to turn aside again in prayer. It was a great vision, but in reality it never worked. It is doubtful how many people ever went to church on weekdays even in previous centuries, and now many churches of all denominations are closed on weekdays, unless they happen to house a café or a toddler group. In fact, if you want to go somewhere for daily prayer, you are more likely to find it in a mosque than in a church. So how are we going to get a rhythm of prayer back into the heart of our Christian communities?

1 Provide resources

Many Christians struggle in their day-to-day prayer lives. Some will snatch a few moments to remember their family and friends before God. Others will try to maintain some sort of structure based around Bible reading notes. Neither model taps into the historic breadth and depth of daily prayer, and neither is particularly well suited to people praying together. The Anglican, Roman Catholic and Orthodox traditions have well-developed patterns of daily prayer, however, and, although I can only speak from experience of the first of these, it seems to me that they are sometimes too well developed. Variety, as they say, is the spice of life, but trying to find your way around the lectionary reading schemes and seasonal calendars of the historic churches is not for the faint-hearted or the uninitiated. If you have never used these patterns of prayer before, the easiest approach is probably to use one of the websites offering daily prayer, which does all the work for you by selecting the right readings and prayers for the day and the season.[28]

In recent years, the upsurge of interest in new ways of being church, which has fused with the rediscovery and reinvention of monastic spirituality, has produced a wealth of new and relatively simple daily prayer resources. In the Community of Aidan and Hilda one of our most popular books has been Ray Simpson's *Prayer Rhythms for Busy People*.[29] This slim pocket-sized book offers daily prayer for morning, noon, evening and night, themed around the seven days of the week. Psalms and Bible readings are printed in the text. For those who want more variety, *Lindisfarne Liturgies* and the four-part *Celtic Prayer Book* by the same author and publisher offer a host of seasonal variations and prayers for special occasions. There are also excellent resources available from the Northumbria Community, the Iona Community, the 24–7 Prayer movement (see *Punk Monk*, mentioned in Chapter 1) and, from America, material from Shane Claiborne and the Simple Way. Any of these will give you enough to get started on daily prayer in simple, engaging and sustainable ways.

2 Gather a core group

Joining together in a rhythm of prayer is one of the three core elements which are essential for creating community. It does not take much imagination, therefore, to see that the best way to do this is to gather a core group of people who will commit themselves to meet for daily prayer. Realistically, because of the unavoidable demands of our 21st-century lifestyles, the core gathering will probably be a minority within any church or Christian group. The key to making it work is simplicity, which is one of the three life-giving principles we explored in Chapter 2, about sharing a Way of Life. Another important point is that while quite a lot of Christians are not very comfortable praying aloud with others, these simple patterns of corporate prayer make it much easier. If you can begin by saying someone else's words, it gradually becomes easier to say aloud a few words of your own at an appropriate point. Liturgy is a much-overlooked resource in helping people to pray.

First of all, then, we need to find out what times of day work best for people. Perhaps we need to have an early time of prayer for people to drop into on their way to work. After all, many people seem able to fit in an early morning run or gym session, so why not 20 or 30 minutes for prayer? Another good time might be just after 9am, for people returning from the school run. For those not at work, a midday prayer time might be best. Evening prayer might need to fit a time when people can drop in on the way home from work, or there might be a mid-evening service of Night Prayer for those who have long days. Clearly, different times of day will suit different groups and the key is to find what fits your own setting. In my experience, retired people are often better able to make up the core group because their days can be more flexible. There is a big challenge in many Western churches to reach and keep younger people, but while we do that, we must not overlook or undervalue the huge contribution that older people can make.

The second necessity is to keep the prayer time simple. While we do not want to fall into a dull mechanical routine, the essence of this kind of rhythmic daily prayer is a degree of predictability. We come to a familiar place at a familiar time and use familiar words in order to make it easier to step out of the pressing pace of our lives and create a space in which we can meet with God. As a vicar I worked for liked to say, 'liturgy is the menu, not the minutes'. In other words, these set forms of prayer give us a shape and structure into which God is able to pour his Spirit. When that happens, there will be more than enough life and creativity to prevent us having to reinvent the wheel every time we pray.

With that in mind, our aim is to set up a comfortable and accessible place to pray, whether in a church or elsewhere. Seating should be comfortable and should not be set out in rows, so that we have a sense of being together. Oddly enough, the choir pews in older churches can be quite appropriate because people can sit facing each other – although some seat padding might come in useful. It is good to have a visual focal point. We often use three candles representing the Trinity, which can be lit to start the prayer time and extinguished at the end. Icons such as Rublev's famous image of the Trinity, inspired by the story of Abraham's three visitors (see Genesis 18), are also popular. You might want to use objects which symbolise your local community. In the Open Gate chapel on Holy Island, the cross is made out of a huge piece of driftwood from the shore, and it rests on a bed of pebbles and rocks from the same place. Even though you are indoors, it speaks of the natural world outside. These are just a few ideas, and, if you are a creative person or you know others who are, you will have no difficulty in coming up with something inspiring to help you focus as you pray.

The idea is to create an environment in which people can simply come in, sit down, take a few moments to gather their thoughts, and begin to pray. If everything is kept as simple and orderly as possible, there is no need to spend time getting ready, as you might do with a normal church service. The only stage directions should be to guide people to the right day of the week if you are using a prayer book like one of the ones recommended above, to share out the Bible readings, and, if you are going to pray a psalm together, to explain how this will be done.

Do not be discouraged if you find yourself praying with only a handful of people or sometimes even on your own. Remember that Jesus said something very famous about what happens when two or three gather together. Remember too that if you are doing it as part of a larger vision of Christian community, of the kind we have been exploring, even if you do find yourself praying alone, you are still praying with the rest of your community, and they will be conscious that at certain times of day someone will be praying in their place of prayer. A very valuable byproduct of this is that closed church buildings get reopened: in my experience, when that happens, people tend to wander in, and they may not be Christians. My church has quite a small congregation scattered over a very congested part of London, so getting a core group together for prayer is not easy. As a result, I often find myself praying alone in church, but that does not stop me meeting people.

A couple of years ago, I was a little late walking out of my house to go to evening prayer. The church car park was normally empty at that time of day but on this occasion a white van was parked there, with its driver walking on to the church grass. Unfortunately, where I live, this normally means they are either going to dump rubbish or looking for a place to relieve themselves! 'Excuse me,' I said. 'Can I help you?'

'I'm a Muslim,' the man said. 'I'm just looking for a place to put down my mat and pray. Is it OK if I do it here?'

'Listen,' I replied, 'it's my evening prayer time, too. I'm going into the church to pray and you're very welcome to come in. I know we pray in different ways but I'll be at the front and you can put your mat down and pray on the carpet at the back.'

'Are you serious?' the man replied. 'I've never been inside a church before. Are you sure it's OK for me to pray there?'

'Of course,' I said. 'Come on in.'

His name turned out to be Adam, which had a certain symbolic resonance, and I'd like to think that, as two different spiritual offspring of Abraham prayed under the same roof in their different ways, God heard both our prayers and it did something to bring a divided human race a little closer together.

On another day a stranger joined me while she waited to go to see a counsellor who lives opposite, and recently a Hindu woman sat in church during Morning Prayer after dropping her daughter off at the Montessori nursery in our hall. God has put a spiritual receiver into everyone. When we find people places where they can pray, we find ourselves creating community.

3 Take it in turns to pray

You can see the problem with all this already. We are saying that a shared rhythm of prayer is one of the essential elements for creating community and that, contrary to many of our modern expectations, personal prayer in the Bible and the early church was seen as the individual outworking of communal prayer. Having a core group of people who meet to pray daily therefore becomes the heartbeat of a living Christian community, setting the rhythm for each individual, wherever they may be. The problem is that today it is often extremely difficult to get people together to pray in any numbers. But there is an answer, and it turns out to be that much-maligned item of administration in churches up and down the land – the rota!

This might sound like a complete cop out. We start with the vision of a rhythm of prayer which is the beating heart of the church, and we end up with individuals signing their name on a list. So let's take a step back, because this has a very inspiring precedent.

According to an ancient Celtic book called *The Annals of Ulster*, the great monastery of Bangor in Northern Ireland was founded by St Comgall in the mid-sixth century. A former soldier, Comgall was no soft touch as a spiritual leader and demanded some of the highest standards of commitment of any Celtic community in Ireland. That only seemed to attract people, and the histories tell us that, when he died in AD602, 3000 people lived under his direction. Bangor was famous for the singing in its worship and, not content with praying seven times a day, the community began a practice known as the *laus perennis* or 'perpetual praise'. Over a period of centuries, praise and prayer were offered to God from Bangor 24 hours a day, seven days a week, 365 days a year. It sounds impossible but in fact we know exactly how they did it. As late as the twelfth century, St Bernard of Clairvaux described how at Bangor 'the solemnization of divine offices was kept up by companies, who relieved each other in succession, so that not for one moment day and night was there an intermission of their devotions'. There you have it: they used a rota. The same is true of the hundred years of prayer started in the 18th century by the Moravian Christians, led by Count Nicholas Zinzendorf, which so significantly influenced John Wesley.

It may well be that people cannot find time in their schedules to meet together to pray more than once or twice a week, but if twelve people can manage half an hour once a week to come to your church or place of prayer, then the vital core of prayer has been established twice daily outside of Sundays. Once it is in place, it is much easier to encourage others to join in when they can.

It would not be right to leave this aspect of establishing a rhythm of prayer without mentioning the extraordinary phenomenon of the 24–7 Prayer movement, which began when a church group that had reached a plateau in its mission, ministry and spirituality took the tremendous step of faith of trying to pray continuously for a month. The story has been told in full elsewhere,[30] but not only did this continuous prayer transform them, it also inspired other people all over the world to try to do the same thing. In autumn 2011, with the same sense of frustration in the life and ministry of our church, and still feeling the aftershocks of the London riots which had left shops burned out and a local resident dead in the street only a mile away, I set up our own modest 24-hour prayer marathon. I was reasonably confident that enough people would sign up to fill all the one-hour prayer slots, but nothing could have prepared me for the impact it had on those who took part.

Here are some of the comments from the 'Reflections' book to which people were invited to contribute as they left after their prayer time.

> The hour went quickly. I could have done with another one really. It was so easy to pray.

> 11.55pm. An hour that absolutely rushed by – and I don't think I had finished all the prayers I intended to say.

> 3am. On with thanks and praise now… I find it's nearly 4am already.

> A special short hour where time seems to stop so you can thank God for everything and pray for the less fortunate.

People prayed for the church, the borough, the wider world and their own needs, and most spoke of an exceptional sense of being in God's presence. What was also strikingly encouraging was the evidence of vision being lifted and renewed. One person wrote of their conviction that 'God wants us to succeed in fulfilling our mission statement [to be a Christian community committed to praying, welcoming, and growing] and will give us the will, capacity, and spirit to do so.' Another reflected that 'being a part of Prayer 24 shows that together we can bring a bigger picture and with each other's help we can achieve greatness.'

The thread that runs through all these responses is that suddenly prayer was *easy*, and one of the reasons for that was the sense that we were not just praying on our own but in a shared endeavour with each other. In other words, we sensed that we were a community in prayer. In one weekend we were transformed from a church which struggled to pray to a church which had discovered hidden wells of prayer, and the streams were starting to flow. As I write, we are gearing up for another 24 hours of prayer and one member of the church has already told me to reserve her a double slot from midnight till 2am!

We are emphatically not a church where people flock to prayer meetings but what I see unmistakably emerging in the last year is a community of prayer. In 2012 London hosted an amazing Olympic Games. There were sprinters, there were marathon runners and there were relay runners. They all went the distance and crossed the finish line. Praying by rota is not inferior to having everyone praying together at once. It's just different. As the baton is passed from one person to another, there is a sense of teamwork and momentum, and together, as Paul wrote, we finish the race and keep the faith (2 Timothy 4:7).

4 Take advantage of technology

The first Christians were early adopters of a new cutting-edge development in information technology. This hand-held device enabled them to carry large documents around with them and access any part of them almost immediately. It was called a book. Until then, most people had written on papyrus scrolls which were large and heavy, like a roll of wallpaper, and very difficult to use if you wanted to look up something in the middle. Books, with their much smaller individual pages, were starting to be used by architects and engineers to carry technical information. The Christians were among the first people to use books for serious writing as well, writing which they would soon regard as scripture.

The problem we have run into again and again in trying to establish a rhythm of prayer is that of keeping people in touch with one another when it is physically difficult to meet face to face. In the 21st century we have better equipment for doing this than at any other time in history. Mobile phone text messages and Tweets[31] can easily be turned into the third-millennium equivalent of the traditional church bell, summoning people to prayer wherever they are. 'Morning Bell' is the name of a Facebook page, written by teacher, poet and artist Ian Adams, which offers a simple daily meditation and prayer focus. A church in my area took a rather more low-tech approach several years ago when, throughout Lent, members pledged to stop and pray the Lord's Prayer wherever they were at 8 o'clock every morning. This is a very simple example of setting up a rhythm of prayer, and a text or Tweet would be the ideal reminder.

Some members of the Community of Aidan and Hilda in Australia have taken this a stage further by partnering up to pray together by phone. They take it in turns to call each other, put their phones on to Speaker so that their hands are free to turn the pages of their prayer books, and, in a moment, they dissolve the distances across a very large country. Using Skype or a similar online phone and/or video conferencing utility would make it possible for a group of people to come together for daily prayer at the click of a mouse. We have great resources available to us at very little cost, so let's be creative in using them.

5 Create a cycle of prayer

Writing to the newly founded church in Thessalonica, Paul urges the believers within a few lines both to 'encourage one another and build up each other' and 'always [to] seek to do good to one another' (1 Thessalonians 5:11, 15). Praying for one another is one of the most basic ways of doing this, but it is easy to be distracted from our good intentions. A daily prayer list or cycle of prayer enables you to pray regularly for all the other people who are following the Way of Life, and is a great source of strength. It is one of the things which binds together a dispersed community like the Community of Aidan and Hilda. I have mentioned already how immensely encouraging it is to know that on a given day of the month nearly 300 people across the world will be praying for me. It is always a special moment to unite a face with a name, when I have perhaps been praying for that person for over five years but have never met them before. Just think how strong that support will be in a local church context where people do meet face to face. Just think of the potential it raises for people to help one another to hear from God.

If we are open to this, it is surprising how often, when we pray for someone, God leads us to pray in a different way than we intended. Sometimes a stray thought will come into our mind which seems particularly relevant to that person at that time. When I was a youth worker a girl in my group walked up to me one evening and said, 'You've got a problem and I've got a Bible verse for you.' She was right, although I had said nothing to her or to anyone else, and you won't be surprised to know that the passage of scripture in her reference spoke words of encouragement which were exactly what I needed. Using a cycle of prayer to pray for one another day by day puts us in a place where God can drop in these inspired thoughts, which can be hugely helpful if we gain in confidence in sharing them with one another.

If the aim of living our Way of Life, supported and encouraged by our Soul Friend, is to connect more deeply with God and to connect God more deeply with the whole of life, then prayer must sink deep into the heart of everything we do because it is the means by which the oxygen of the Spirit energises our minds and bodies. A daily rhythm of prayer connects us with God, and as we pray with others it produces a virtuous circle which both creates and expresses community. This is a wonderful vision, but without action it will remain just a beautiful daydream. It's time to get started, and how to do that is the subject of the final chapter.

Chapter 5

Taking the first steps

In the previous chapters we have explored what it means to share a Way of Life, journey with a Soul Friend and join in a rhythm of prayer. I have suggested that these three elements are ancient tools which need to be rediscovered and transplanted from their first-millennium origins into our third-millennium setting because they are the essential elements from which we create meaningful and lasting Christian community. Through them we are better equipped to connect more deeply with God and one another, and to connect God with the whole of life. In exploring these things, I have shared something of my own journey of discovery and what I have learned as part of this work in progress.

I began by using the image of Eric Shipton's groundbreaking expedition to Mount Everest, which, though it did not succeed in putting a climber on top of the mountain, opened up a way to the summit for others to follow. For various reasons Shipton never returned to Everest. By contrast, I've had the opportunity to embark in person upon the kind of project that this book describes. In classic mountaineering terms, you might say that our Christian community in West London has already broken trail and established camps on the mountain, but the summit still lies ahead of us. In this final chapter I want to try to draw a picture of how this model of Christian community might work in practice and, most importantly, to help others to take their first steps on the journey. If you're fit and strong you might well overtake us on the way, and if you do, I'll be cheering you all the way to the top!

Sketching out the destination

When I first began thinking through the ideas which have ended up in this book, I was propelled by the conviction that a large part of the contemporary appeal of Celtic spirituality is the parallels that exist between the social contexts of the first and third millennia. It has often been suggested that monasticism originated in no small part as a response to a corrupt society and a compromised church, when for the first time it became socially advantageous to be a Christian after the Roman Emperor Constantine had adopted the faith in the fourth century. By contrast, the Irish church, from which the Celtic mission sprang, was never within the Roman Empire, and this Celtic mission proved to be highly effective in evangelising pagan post-Roman Europe. The need to reach out with the gospel to a predominantly non-Christian society while at the same time renewing the church forms a close parallel with our present situation.

At the time, I felt that the best way forward for anyone who wanted to run with this vision would be to start from scratch with a genuinely fresh expression of church. For over a thousand years, our predominant model of church, in more or less any denomination you care to name, has been that of the congregation, not the community, with Sunday worship as its main focal point. In recent years the weaknesses of this way of thinking have become more and more apparent, yet the alternatives are not easy to embrace. Some existing churches have tried to go over to the 'cell' model where the primary unit is a dozen or so people meeting weekly in homes, with less frequent larger gatherings.[32] This is a truly radical and exciting vision but I think it is fair to say that it has not been adopted by a large number of churches, not least because it takes a huge amount of energy to re-engineer a traditional church to operate in this way. Most of my experience has been in helping churches to adopt new values and practices in mission, ministry and worship, and I know that it is a fairly slow process if you are determined to take the majority of people with you on the journey. I have no time at all for the brash approach we used to hear, which claimed that 'sometimes you have to empty a church in order to fill it'. What kind of shepherd increases their flock by butchering half of the existing sheep – especially when the sheep don't belong to them to start with? For these two reasons I initially thought that the best way forward would be to start a new kind of church from scratch.

There is no doubt that we need all kinds of new churches to express the life and message of Jesus in fresh, contemporary and creative ways, and, if the ideas in this book help and inspire you to start one of these churches, I will be delighted. Nevertheless that is not the road I have taken, for the simple reason that I believe God has called me in a different direction, and having embarked on that journey I have come to realise that some of my early assumptions were wrong. At one stage I did think that if I was going to put this vision into practice, I would need to move out of my current job and start a new church, but as soon as I began, behind the scenes, to explore this idea, I was confronted by doors shutting firmly in my face. It rapidly became clear that these were not obstacles to be overcome but God's emphatic way of telling me that he wanted me to stay put. Once I had grasped that, it was a short step to grasping a new challenge. If this vision of a different way of doing and being church was really from God, it had to be something I could work out where God had put me, as part of a process of transition in an existing church. I think it can be, and therefore, while I will be delighted if material in this book can be used by those of you starting new churches, my focus will be on the hundreds of thousands of existing Christians in existing churches who have the urge we have already mentioned: to connect more deeply with God and each other, and to connect God more deeply with the whole of life, right where they are.

Let's suppose that we succeed in creating the kind of community I have been outlining in this book, with a Way of Life, a network of Soul Friends and a rhythm of prayer. What will that look like if it is worked through in an existing church? Will it mean that everyone has to commit to it 100 per cent? If so, there will be little chance of achieving our aim. Will it mean having a divided church, with an inner core committed to community living, in tension with another group of people who have not done so? Clearly that will not be good either. In fact, when we go back to the early Celtic monasteries like Hilda's community at Whitby, we find that they contained a broad variety of people who related to the community in different but equally valid ways. There were the brothers and sisters living under committed vows. Many were single but, surprisingly to our eyes, and I think very refreshingly, some of them were married. There were lots of other people worshipping with the community and influenced by its values but not living under the full discipline of the community rule. There were doubtless also many travellers and visitors, passing through and enjoying hospitality, who were not members of the village of God, and it is highly likely that some of these will not have been Christians at all. This gives us a clear model for Christian community today.

Using the terminology I'm familiar with as a life member of the Community of Aidan and Hilda, and adding some new terms from day-to-day church life, I suggest that our new type of Christian community might be made up of four different types of people, each relating to it in a different but equally valid way.

- **'Voyagers'**: These are people fully committed to the journey of living out the Way of Life in relationship with their Soul Friend and committed to the community's rhythm of prayer. They will have made this commitment in a public act of dedication and will renew it annually.
- **'Explorers'**: As the name suggests, these are people who are exploring what it means to live by the Way of Life. This will involve a period of a least a year during which they start to build a relationship with a Soul Friend and work out their personal and practical application of the Way of Life.
- **'Believers'**: Jesus said, 'Anyone who comes to me I will never drive away' (John 6:37) and 'If any of you put a stumbling block before one of these little ones who believe in me, it would be better for you if a great millstone were hung around your neck

and you were thrown into the sea' (Mark 9:42). In seeking to enable people to go deeper in their walk with God, it is vital that we do not create barriers which prevent them from being part of their local Christian community. The term 'believers' therefore describes those Christians who are committed to the life of their church but, for whatever reason, choose not to commit personally to following the Way of Life or having a Soul Friend. The whole argument of this book is that both are excellent and beneficial things, but neither is essential to salvation and any Christian community must welcome people to be part of it at their own level.

- **'Seekers'**: In Acts, Luke tells us a remarkable thing about the first Christians in Jerusalem who met in the temple: 'None of the rest dared to join them, but the people held them in high esteem. Yet more than ever believers were added to the Lord, great numbers of both men and women' (Acts 5:13–14). Many of the great Celtic saints felt a call to solitude; yet, wherever they went, people were drawn to them and they ended up gathering those people into communities. Any healthy Christian community will therefore both attract and welcome those who are just passing through, or who want at this time to stay on the fringes, or who are genuinely outsiders looking in to see what Christianity might be all about.

Too often we have thought of Christian community in terms of types of activity. At various times in history, people have tried to create deeper levels of belonging and discipleship by trying to live together and share everything in common on the model of the early Christians in Jerusalem. For two good reasons this has been, and will only ever be, a model of community for the minority of Christians. In the first place it is very hard, and there is much wisdom to be gained from traditional monastic communities concerning the disciplines and practices required to make it work. Secondly, and perhaps more importantly, it was never practised or taught elsewhere in the early church. Paul did not teach the churches he planted to live this way and nor, as far as we know, did any of the other apostles. In every age there will be Christians who are called to follow this radical path, and some of today's new monastic communities are again experimenting with it, but it is not the only way to live in true community.

The other common approach to creating Christian community is to look creatively at all kinds of ways to bring our faith to bear on day-to-day life and to find ways of bringing people together. From a historical perspective, Ian Bradley looks at how the Celtic churches did this, while Ray Simpson offers a variety of wildly imaginative and inspiring ways in which we might do it today.[33] From my perspective, for these visions to become an enduring reality, what matters is the quality of connection with God and each other that underlies them; and to earth this connection, a Way of Life, a network of Soul Friends and a rhythm of prayer are essential. Without these, we run the risk of creating yet another flurry of activity which will ultimately burn out because it lacks the quality of relationships to sustain it.

Getting started with a Way of Life

So you've read this far and you're convinced enough to want to put into practice what you've read. How do you begin to live by a Way of Life?

I said at the start of Chapter 2 that a Way of Life is a simple summary set of guidelines outlining what it means in practice to live a God-centred life in a particular time or setting. Paul tells us that 'all scripture is inspired by God and is useful for teaching, for reproof, for correction, and for training in righteousness, so that everyone who belongs to God may be proficient, equipped for every good work' (2 Timothy 3:16–17). Christians vary over precisely what they believe about the inspiration and authority of scripture, but pretty well all of us agree that we're not at liberty to change the actual text of the Bible, however much we may disagree about how to interpret it and put it into practice. Only scripture, then, is unchanging. Any Way of Life of any community, no matter how prayerfully and thoughtfully it is set out, will always be secondary and changeable by its very nature, because its purpose is to help people distil the teachings of scripture and live them relevantly and practically in their particular circumstances. We can therefore follow any number of perfectly valid Ways of Life. The issue is finding the right one.

In the Anglican tradition, to which I belong, we try to allow three factors to shape our beliefs, behaviour, doctrines and decisions. These are scripture, the written word of God; tradition, meaning the wisdom of Christians down the centuries; and reason, bringing our own thinking and experience to bear. In theory it would be possible to come up with a Way of Life from scratch, simply by reflecting on scripture, but in practice that is not how most people do it, not least because there are few of us who feel we know the Bible thoroughly enough to do it competently. Instead most people who begin to live by a Way of Life adopt one which has been worked out by others, drawing on their greater experience and insights. Even the innovative Boiler Room communities described in *Punk Monk* took five years of careful thought and prayer to work out their Way of Life and it is clear how conscious Pete Greig and Andy Freeman are of their debt to the historic Christian communities, especially the Celtic ones, which inspired them.

The way in which people end up joining dispersed Christian communities such as the Community of Aidan and Hilda is normally in response to a sense that the values and spirituality and Way of Life of the community strike a chord with them. No matter how initially challenging the Way of Life may seem, they have an instinctive sense that somehow it fits. Therefore my recommendation to anyone who wants to begin living by a Way of Life is to adopt one that has already been developed and tested by others. If the one set out in this book does not feel appropriate, go and research what other communities have to offer until you find the one that connects with you. Whichever Way of Life you feel God calling you to adopt, use the process set out at the end of Chapter Two to work out how you will apply it in your life.

Let me stress again that there is no need to hurry. Do not try to do too much at once: remember that you have the rest of your life to refine it. Find yourself a Soul Friend (more about how to do that in a moment) and go through it with them. My experience with the Community of Aidan and Hilda is that the one-year minimum of the Explorer period is vital in terms of working out what should and should not be in our Way of Life and then beginning to road-test it in day-to-day living. We also encourage people to review their Way of Life once a year, and this can be a time to make changes to our personal application based on alterations in our circumstances, growth in our understanding, or our response to something that God is currently showing us or calling us to do. The Way of Life set out in this book is adapted from that of the Community of Aidan and Hilda, so, if it resonates with you, you can find details at the end of this book of how to contact the Community. Our nature as a dispersed community means that we are fully focused on helping people to live out their Way of Life wherever they are, so there is plenty of help and advice available.

Getting started with Soul Friendship

Probably the most common question we are asked in the Community of Aidan and Hilda is 'Can you help me find a Soul Friend?' In response, we have developed a fledgling network of Soul Friend Advisers to help people, and we are also in the process of producing some training materials. You may already know someone who has a link with spiritual direction or you may have contact with a religious community whose members offer this kind of ministry. For many of us, however, this will be a whole new area and we may not think we know anyone who can help us. Don't be discouraged, because the answer may be closer than you think.

In his first book on Soul Friendship, Ray Simpson provides an enormously practical and useful chapter on 'Choosing and changing a Soul Friend'.[34] Please notice the title because it is important. A

Soul Friend may not necessarily be for life. For all kinds of reasons we may be accompanied by a particular Soul Friend for a period of our spiritual journey but then make a change. Perhaps it is no longer practical to meet because of distance, or maybe the relationship has simply run its course and we need to find someone else to help us on the next stage of our journey. There is nothing wrong with this and such changes are perfectly amicable. The only things to keep in mind are that our priority is to be led by God, and that changing our Soul Friend because what they are saying is challenging to us is not a good idea! The strict eight-century Irish monk Maelruain advised in the Rule of Tallaght that, in looking for a Soul Friend, 'you should seek out the fire which will most fiercely burn, that is, which will spare you the least'.[35] That kind of spiritual commando training is not where most of us will want to start, but we should note the important principle there.

Ray Simpson suggests a helpful checklist for anyone trying to find a Soul Friend, designed to help us think through what kind of person we are looking for.

- Male or female?
- Older than you are?
- An ordained minister?
- A member of a religious community?
- Rooted within a particular Christian tradition – for example, Roman Catholic, evangelical, Orthodox, charismatic, and so on?
- A trained spiritual director?
- Able to be contacted outside of scheduled meetings?
- Available by phone, email and/or online chat?
- Formal or informal in style?

Ray also recommends thinking about what we want to get out of the meetings with our Soul Friend. For example:

- Help in listening to God
- Help with spiritual growth and understanding

- Help with processing our emotions and inner life
- Help with making important decisions

Work through the list, being as specific as you can with each of these points, and write down any other factors which seem important.

Next, revisit the four basic qualities of a Soul Friend:

- Listening skills
- Reflectiveness
- Prayerfulness
- Dedication to trying to walk closely with God

Write a list of everyone you know who seems to have these four qualities in some measure. Now compare that list with your profile of your ideal Soul Friend. How closely do any of the points fit? It may be that you already know someone who could be a Soul Friend to you. Even if they do not have previous experience in this area, you may be surprised by how open they are to a request to meet with you a few times a year to help you think through and pray about your own walk with God.

You may not find a Soul Friend quickly, but remember that it should not be rushed. Be aware, too, that you have joined in a process of rediscovering ancient spiritual practices which have been neglected by much of the church for over 1000 years. Don't be surprised if it is not immediately easy to find someone with experience in this area who is not already overloaded with lots of other enquirers. That said, don't lose sight of the fact that you are on a journey with God, a journey into new places to make new discoveries, and even at the start of this journey it will not always be clear what is around the corner. Jesus spoke directly to this journey of faith when he said, 'Ask, and it will be given to you; search, and you will find; knock, and the door will be opened for you… If you then, who are evil, know how to give good gifts to your children, how much more will your Father in heaven give good things to those who ask him!' (Matthew

7:7–11). Proverbs 18:24 says, 'A true friend sticks closer than one's nearest kin.' A Soul Friend is undoubtedly a good thing, so, if you feel that God is calling you to seek one, be assured that he will lead you to the right person in his own time.

Getting started with a rhythm of prayer

There's much less to be said about this, because most us probably already have some kind of personal prayer rhythm, even if it's not as regular as we might like it to be. From there it will simply be a case of looking back to the ideas and principles in Chapter Four and deciding how they will work most effectively for us as individuals and for the group of people we want to pray with.

As ever, don't be afraid to start simple and start small. Many of us have busy lives so making short regular prayer stops is far better than trying to commit to something longer and finding that we either can't spare the time or are rushing to get on to the next thing. The ideal is to set aside some time in the morning and evening, but don't worry if you only manage one or the other at first, or, if a small group is trying to meet to pray, you can only get together a couple of days a week. Part of my weekly pattern is to meet for Morning Prayer on Mondays and Fridays with a friend who is minister of a church on the other side of Ealing. We take it in turns to make the morning commute but I can honestly say that, having done it for some years now, it really makes a difference. As two fellow members of the Community of Aidan and Hilda, it is a very positive and real way for us to express the life of our community. Do what you can, not what you can't.

One final point about a daily prayer rhythm is a small warning not to become legalistic about it. Keen Christians down the ages have sometimes taken patterns and turned them into prisons. Don't forget that we are under grace and not under law (Romans 6:14–15). If you miss a prayer stop during the day, don't try to make it up later, just move on to the next one. God knew that you were too busy or too distracted to turn up but he's endlessly patient and simply waits for you at the next stop. The point of having prayer stops throughout the day is not to pray a certain number of psalms or get through a Bible reading scheme or tick off names on a prayer list. The purpose is to connect God with the whole of our life. If we miss one opportunity during the day, we can't repeat that section of time, so the best thing to do, without condemnation, is to move on to the next meeting with God.

As a footnote to this, I have been very impressed by the way another faith handles this issue. For Muslims the set times of prayer are much more strictly and formally observed, but just like us, they face the problem of how to fit these times into inflexible schedules. One Saturday I was in a balti house in Acton, not far from my home, waiting for a takeaway. I could tell that the staff were Muslim because of the massive poster of Mecca on the wall. As they dashed back and forth, cooking curry and feeding naan bread in and out of the tandoor oven, the hour of prayer arrived. With a shop full of customers and gas rings burning everywhere, they could hardly stop, but I noticed two of them pause for a moment, nod to one another, turn briefly to face the picture of Mecca, and then carry on cooking. Some people will dismiss this as ritual and superstition. I think it's practical faith in action. Consciously seeking to connect with God even for a moment is better than not connecting with God at all. Pray as you can, not as you can't. The great thing about connecting with God, especially when we find ways to do it with other people, is that the more the connection is made, the more we want it to continue.

Suggestions for church leaders

One of the reasons I had the confidence to write this book is that, over the years, I have talked to many church leaders from different denominations about the challenges we all face, and have explored some of the ideas I've been setting out here. Through those conversations I realised that I might be on to something valid. If you are a church leader, then in many ways this book is particularly for you, and this section offers a number of thoughts for those of you wanting to know how to put it all into practice and work at creating community where you are.

1 'Everything rises and falls on leadership'[36]

That sounds like a strong statement, but in reality we will quickly find that we cannot take other people anywhere that we are not going ourselves. One of the greatest privileges in church leadership is that we are in a position where we have the freedom and authority to implement a vision which we believe comes from God. I also like the definition of leadership which says that the leader is the person who knows what the next step is. We may not be able to see much further ahead than that, but in any group the one who knows what to do next is the leader, whether or not they have the formal title.

This came home to me very forcibly several years ago when I started trying to introduce the idea and practice of Soul Friendship into our church. I had explained about Soul Friendship and I had a group of people who were interested. I thought at the time that the best way forward would be to help people learn some of the necessary skills, especially listening; then we would see who might have emerging gifts in this area. I bought a training course on listening and we got together to watch the DVD and do the learning exercises. So far, so good – except that it wasn't. As we tried to schedule the second session, about half the group either wanted to drop out or made it clear that they were just not very enthusiastic. To be honest, the course was not quite as good as we had hoped, but as I reflected further I recognised the real problem – I was asking them to commit to exploring something they had only ever heard about in theory and had never seen in practice.

That autumn I had a few days' annual retreat on Holy Island. As I travelled to Northumbria, this setback in the vision to create community through a Way of Life, Soul Friendship and a rhythm of prayer was at the front of my mind. Holy Island is a great place to walk and think. Within a few minutes you can be out of the village and the inhabited part of the island, crossing open fields to paths into the sand dunes which lead you out on to the beaches and coves. At the north-east corner of the island stands a strange tall, steep, white pyramid. It's a ship mark, built before the days of radar as an aiming point and navigation guide for vessels negotiating the reefs and sands round the island. As I walked, I began to sense God speaking to me in my thoughts. I was reminded that if I wanted to help people move into the next stage of what I believed God was calling us to, I would need to exercise some spiritual leadership. I was the only person among them who knew what Soul Friendship really was because I had had a Soul Friend for nearly ten years. Therefore, if they were ever going to see what it really was, I would have to model it to them. This was a more than daunting prospect. My previous Soul Friend and my current one are both people of maturity and experience in Christian leadership, gifted with great insight. I also knew a number of other people involved in this ministry, and they were all exceptionally gifted in terms of both listening to God and listening to others. Whenever anyone asked me if I would be a Soul Friend to someone in the Community, I always used to say that I felt my own gifts lay elsewhere.

All the time I was thinking this, the clean white ship mark was standing out in front of me and getting closer with every step. As I arrived at its base, I sensed God nudging me to have a good look at it. Close up, the white paint was dirty and peeling. 'Look how battered and unimpressive it is when you get close up,' he seemed to be saying. 'Yet it still points beyond itself and guides others effectively.' I got the point. I may not be as gifted as other people when it comes to Soul Friendship, but I knew more about it first-hand than anyone else in the church where God had placed me and called me to care for its people. God seemed to be saying that my shortcomings were not a problem to him. 'You know that you cannot teach others unless you continue to learn. You cannot grow others unless you continue to grow. You cannot grow unless you reach beyond yourself.'

I went back to London and got back in touch with everyone. I explained that I'd made a mistake. It was bit like what happens when you're climbing a mountain. A very important skill is that of route finding, the ability to be able to spot the best line through an area of broken ground or the most climbable line of weakness when a crag bars the way. Sometimes the only way to find the best route is to try climbing up somewhere. If it turns out to be a dead end, you just have to climb down and try another way. I'd led people up a dead end and it was time to try another way. I told them that the best way to learn about Soul Friendship was to experience it, and therefore, since I had found great benefit over the years in meeting with my Soul Friend, I was offering to meet with anyone who would like to spend time talking about how their Christian life was going. As I have described earlier in this book, that turned out to be one of the best decisions I ever made. When it comes to creating this kind of community, there is no room for the authoritarian 'I say "jump", you say "how high?"' models of leadership which are still all too common in the Christian church. Yet leadership matters very much indeed because we can only lead other people on a path we are already walking.

2 Vision must be owned and earthed

There are plenty of good programmes around which address lots of important areas of discipleship and church life, but this is not one of them. Think back to the way the Celtic Christian communities probably grew and multiplied across the country. A group would be sent out to found a new community somewhere else. They would almost certainly take with them the Way of Life and prayer patterns of their parent community, but it's highly likely that, as the new community settled and as its members and leaders grew in their walk with God, these things would have evolved and taken on a life of their own. The seventh-century community founded on Holy Island would have brought with them what they learned on Iona, all no doubt attributed to Columba. Within a short time it would have become known to newcomers as the Way of Aidan, and, as Aidan trained and sent out others, his practices would have become known as the Way of Hilda or of any of the many other new community founders. If we could have compared all these communities side by side, we would have found many differences of detail and local variations, but also a clear family resemblance.

In the same way, as we seek to introduce a Way of Life, a network of Soul Friends and a rhythm of prayer into our churches, we may need to make tweaks and alterations to fit our local circumstances. We may need to change some of the language or refine some parts of the Way of Life. We may need to set up the rhythm of prayer in a way that makes it more accessible for the people we know. All of this will take time and discernment because we are looking for whatever God wants to plant where we are. Don't immediately assume that you can automatically adopt something off the peg. Take the time to find out what is right for you in your setting.

3 Sow the seeds of the vision and keep watering them

In Chapter One I described how I found in Celtic Christianity the answers to real and immediate problems which I was facing in my own church situation. Talking to others over the years has convinced me that I am not alone in facing these challenges. Somebody once said that if you want to get people's attention, you must say something which is beneficial or threatening, or has novelty value. We are not in the business of threatening people and I am inclined to think that the commercially driven 'Celtic revival' of a few years back has now reached its sell-by date. That leaves only one attention grabber – relevance – and I think that these ancient tools for creating community have it in spades.

John Maxwell, whom I quoted above concerning the importance of leadership, has also written at length on how to develop creative thinking in relation to leadership.[37] He suggests that one way to evaluate a new idea is to think of it in terms of all its opposites. We might therefore highlight that we are talking about:

- community, not just congregation
- rhythms of prayer, not just places of worship
- relationships, not just activity
- spiritual life, not just structural maintenance
- organism, not just organisation
- connection, not isolation

Unless you are in a church which allows you to preach at considerable length, the best way to get new ideas across will probably be to run a well-publicised 'Vision Day', making a special effort to invite personally all the people whom you regard as having a significant role in your church. I have also found it useful to end the day with a simple opportunity for response – as basic as a 'yes/no' question such as 'Did you find the ideas inspiring?' All the people who say 'yes' will be your core group to invite to the next stage and to carry the vision forward. For those of you in churches which observe saints' days as part of your worship, there is an added opportunity to use the festivals of the Celtic saints to talk about what they can teach us today. St Aidan's day is at the end of August, St Hilda's day is in November and St Cuthbert's day is in March, so that gives a useful spread across different times of year.

4 Teach about the Way of Life, Soul Friendship and prayer rhythms

If you are in the habit of putting together preaching series, the ten elements of the Way of Life should keep you going for quite a while, and, whether or not people buy into it in full, they will hear all kinds of useful stuff. Once again, it is important to stress that you will need to keep repeating some of the material over and over again. These practices have been ignored by most of the Christian church for most of the last 1000 years, so they will be unfamiliar to a lot of people and will raise a lot of questions.

In terms of resources, Ray Simpson's book *A Pilgrim Way* offers an extensive and deeply insightful commentary on the original form of the Way of Life set out in this book. His more recent set of daily readings, *Waymarks for the Journey*, explores the Way of Life in even greater depth as well as being an excellent resource for individuals and groups to use in daily prayer and reflection.[38] This book is thought-provoking in every way.

Resources on Soul Friendship are a little harder to pin down. There is a lot of material aimed at people involved in spiritual direction, as well as a variety of courses. However, very little of this material is aimed at beginners and many of the courses are long and expensive. Ray's book *Soul Friendship*, mentioned above, is a good way in, although it is now slightly hard to track down. A more recent book, *A Guide for Soul Friends*, recaps some of the material and adds a lot more practical advice.[39]

My own feeling is that a more apprenticeship-based approach is a better way of learning about Soul Friendship, and I'd also suggest that it reflects more closely the culture of the Bible. After all, Peter, James and John never went on a course called 'A Beginners' Guide to being an Apostle' before they got involved in the mission and ministry of Jesus. They got to know Jesus, experienced him at work, and were then taught on the job. The best way, therefore, to learn Soul Friendship is to find your own Soul Friend and reflect upon what they do. As we begin to take the first steps in listening to others and reflecting with them upon what God is doing in their lives, we can then start to refine and increase our skills.

By far the most useful practical handbook I have found is Sue Pickering's *Spiritual Direction: A Practical Introduction*, which does exactly what it says on the front cover.[40] It is a very comprehensive book, written by someone with plenty of hands-on experience. The book also invites the reader to stop and reflect at every stage and provides some very helpful fictionalised dialogues between a Soul Friend and people in a range of different situations. Gordon Jeff's *Spiritual Direction for Every Christian* is another very good introduction, with some thought-provoking material on why spiritual direction should be part of day-to-day church life and not just a specialist ministry.[41] Lastly, specific material on developing listening skills is available from the Acorn Christian Healing Foundation.

5 Invite people regularly to make an initial commitment to the process

You may get the encouragement of finding that a widespread group of people embrace the three elements of community, but it may take longer, with individuals catching the vision one at a time. The threshold seems to be crossed when a person says 'yes' to the invitation to meet for a first exploratory conversation about how their walk with God is going. As part of that first conversation, it is easy to recap the larger vision and invite them to begin working on a personal application of the Way of Life. As this starts to take root, you can then think about getting Explorers together to share the journey and encourage each other.

6 Be clear in your own mind about what you are beginning

Jesus made the obvious point that anyone who sets out to build something will make sure before they begin that they have enough resources to complete the project (Luke 14:28). There is a cost involved in being a disciple and seeking the kingdom of God. I remember someone who had been to an early presentation of some of the material in this book coming to see me to talk further about putting it into practice in his church. He asked me how long it might take, before mentioning that he was going to retire in the next two years. I strongly advised him that it was not really worth starting because he would not have time to see it through.[42]

Before you begin, ask yourself two questions. First, am I sure that God is calling me to do this? Secondly, am I in it for the long haul? Short-termism is the plague of 21st-century British society. Governments and businesses demand immediate returns on their investments. Football managers have to deliver success within a season. Most products that we buy are designed to become obsolete within a few years and be replaced. We might argue that Jesus did not live in an industrial or technologically advanced society, but it cannot be coincidence that many of the images he used for the work of the kingdom were from agriculture and the natural world, where patience as well as skill is required. Community cannot be built on short-term relationships. Research in the Anglican Church has indicated that ministers reach their highest level of effectiveness after being in a place for five to seven years. It is also very interesting to note that some of the largest and most effective churches in Britain are led by people who have been in place for 20 years or more.

It will take time to help people even begin to understand what creating community is all about. It will take time to show them that a Way of Life is truly life-giving and not just another church project. It will take time to show them that sharing their journey with a Soul Friend will be an exercise in encouragement, not embarrassment, and probably even longer to help them see that they could offer this ministry to someone else. It will take time to show them that a rhythm of prayer will bring God's immediacy and energy into their daily lives rather than being just another item on an already overloaded schedule. Ultimately, for those of us in church leadership, the call to create this kind of community is a call to become fathers and mothers in God to the people we lead and serve. 'Who is sufficient for these things?' Paul wrote with some feeling (2 Corinthians 2:16), and we may say exactly the same thing. Yet in the same letter, when personal difficulties were threatening to overwhelm him, Paul also recorded God's answer to that cry: 'My grace is sufficient for you, for power is made perfect in weakness' (12:9). That's why it matters so much to make sure that we know what God is calling us to do, because if he has called us, he will also make sure that we have what we need to see it through. When times get tough, it is that sense of calling which will keep us going.

Some of us will know clearly that we have received a long-term, even lifelong, call to a particular place and group of people, but what about those of us who simply do not know? The story of the Irish saint Finnbarr can help us a lot. Contemporary Biblical scholars such as Tom Wright have helped us to rediscover that the future God intends for us is not to leave earth for ever and go and live in heaven. Rather, when we die, we are to remain with Jesus until the day when God creates the new heavens and the new earth. Celtic Christians had a very literal and down-to-earth belief in resurrection. They believed that the place where they died and were buried would be the place where they would be resurrected in the renewal of all things. It was therefore very important to many of them to find their God-given 'place of resurrection' and live the remainder of their life there.

Finnbarr planted a church at Loch Iree in Ireland and had oversight of several others, but he sensed that this was not to be his place of resurrection and felt that God was leading him to another place, called Gougane Barra, where he founded a new community and established it over many years. One day, two of his former pupils arrived, convinced that God had told them that Gougane Barra was to be their special place of resurrection. Finbarr's reaction was astonishing. Rather than questioning whether they had heard God correctly, or indeed wondering why he had been there so long if the place was meant for someone else, Finbarr simply gave them the place and the community and moved on. In all, throughout his life he founded no fewer than twelve new communities, which must have given a spiritual home to thousands of people, before finding his true place of resurrection in the Irish city of Cork, where the cathedral is dedicated in his name. The lesson from Finbarr is a simple one. If, after genuinely seeking God, we cannot be sure whether he wants us to remain in the place where we are for the long term, just behave as if he did want that. If you sense his call to create community, start doing it where you are and trust God for the future, both for yourself and for the people you seek to lead and serve.

Suggestions for individuals and small groups

What if you're not a church leader but you find yourself drawn to this vision of Christian community and want to try to put it into practice? Obviously you can begin to live this way yourself and you might want to hook up with one of the dispersed Christian communities mentioned previously, in order to belong to a wider network of support and fellowship without compromising your involvement in your local church. A next step, as this belonging becomes rooted and grounded in your own life, would be to talk to the leader or leaders of your church and share what you have discovered, which might inspire them to investigate it themselves. I'm always surprised at how many Christians, in a broad spread of different kinds of churches, lack the confidence to go and speak to their leaders. They assume either that the leaders will be too busy to listen, or that they themselves will be considered too inexperienced or unimportant to be worth listening to. In reality I reckon that most church leaders will be overjoyed if a member of their congregation says they would like to meet to talk about something which has inspired them and helped them grow in their Christian life. All too often, for leaders, a request for an appointment is a prelude to a new problem surfacing, so it will probably make their day!

What if your church leaders are pleased about what you have found but don't feel that this is the direction they should take themselves? There is no reason why you should not get together with a few like-minded friends and set up your own little community group. Anyone can follow a Way of Life wherever they are, so that part will be easy. You can set up ways to pray together using the suggestions in Chapter Four. Finding Soul Friends may be a little more difficult, especially if you are unable to connect with anyone outside your present situation. In that case, remember that God always equips his people with the gifts they need. You could try meeting in pairs, one of you taking the Soul Friend role on one occasion and the next time swapping over. You might also get hold of some of the resources mentioned above in order to develop your skills. Over time, it is likely that one or two people will emerge who have effective gifts in the area of Soul Friendship.

Finally, if you do find yourself in this situation, please tell the leadership of your church what you are doing. That's only courteous but it will also prevent any misunderstandings and any danger of being seen as divisive. Personally I can't imagine many church leaders worth their salt being unhappy to hear that a group of people in their church have got together to pray regularly and support one another in their Christian lives. You could also stress that the values of the Way of Life place a strong emphasis on unity and mission, so your group will be able to serve God more effectively in the mission and ministry of your church.

If the minister or leadership are not happy, you have some tricky decisions to make. You might decide, out of respect for them, not to go ahead, or to join a dispersed community as your way of living out your calling. You might equally consider that your church has no right to control how you live or who you meet with, and go ahead anyway. If that causes friction, it might be a good time to question whether your church is a healthy place to be. It worries me that sincere Christians so often tolerate controlling and abusive leaders. Sometimes it's right to stay because you can change things, but, if that looks unlikely, for your own spiritual well-being it may be time to leave. Make sure, though, that you connect quickly with another church or Christian group. There is no such thing as a solo Christian.

I've described a worst-case scenario, which I suspect will not happen in the majority of situations. It is far more difficult to take the first step than to try to predict where it all might lead. But now you know where you're trying to get to, and you've got a few ideas about how to proceed. It's time to set out. What's stopping you?

Conclusion

I started by comparing creating community with climbing a mountain. That picture is helpful, but only up to a point. Although mountaineering is a pretty serious business (get it wrong and you can end up dead), most people do it for fun. Creating community in the 21st century is far more important than that.

I began with two questions that seem to be confronting Christians and churches everywhere. How do we create, maintain and deepen a genuine and lasting community, and how do we create mature adult disciples of Jesus Christ? Many of our existing church structures and practices do not appear to answer these questions effectively, and those that do seem only to work in particular situations and not for everyone. We need something better.

All over the world, small groups, sometimes identified by the label of 'new monasticism', are going back to the roots of the faith and finding new ways to grow. Belonging to a dispersed Christian community, the Community of Aidan and Hilda, which identifies closely with this movement, I have discovered just how much the first-millennium church in the British Isles has to teach the third-millennium church. We struggle to turn congregations into communities. They started with communities that gathered congregations around themselves. What sustained these communities and held them together was not their common life or the many and various ministries and activities that flowed out from them, but rather three deeply seated values and practices, common to them all. The first was following a shared Way of Life which sought to set out in summary form what it meant in practice to be a Christian in their time and culture. The second was the practice of Soul Friendship whereby every member of the community had a compassionate companion to walk alongside them on their spiritual journey. The third was a rhythm of prayer which punctuated every day, immersing the whole of life in a greater awareness of the presence of God.

The result of practising these three things, as I have discovered over the last ten years, is to be part of a people who have a deepening connection with God and one another, and who are connecting God more and more with every part of their lives. This is what real Christianity is all about, and if by these means we end up knowing God better, and finding more of God at work in our lives, that alone must be worth pursuing.

There is, however, a reason why this vision of Christian community is not merely exciting but also immediately urgent.

When Jesus looked at the people of his day, he saw that 'they were harassed and helpless, like sheep without a shepherd' (Matthew 9:36). This is an Old Testament image for people without leadership, guidance or direction in life. Living as I do in one of the great capital cities of the world, I consider these words as true today as they ever were. Here are some of the things we can see in contemporary Britain.

- Economic uncertainty as capitalism falls into crisis. It has been observed that idolatry always ends in human sacrifice. We have made the market into an idol and now it consumes its followers. Protesters in a cathedral churchyard say there must be a better way, but no one knows what it is.
- Political instability, with a shotgun marriage of two rival parties in Britain, and upheavals elsewhere in Europe. 'Where there is no vision, the people perish' (Proverbs 29:18, KJV), but who can we trust?
- Environmental crisis as the backdrop to all we do. Most of the time we talk about the weather and fail to notice the changing climate. When we do, the need to save money wins over the need to save the planet.

- Moral relativism in which everyone appeals to ethics but, when we press them harder, we find little more than a clash of personal opinions.
- Aggressive atheism which seeks to portray people of faith as not only deluded but actually downright dangerous and therefore to be marginalised in public life.
- Re-emerging racism as the vision of a multicultural society starts to sink back into the sands of suspicion and hatred of those who are different.
- Increasing anger as a result of fear, insecurity and powerlessness, showing itself in a desire to lash out at whoever obstructs or simply irritates us.

We've been heading this way for a long time. While the London Olympic Games gave us much to celebrate, I am not convinced that their wonderful feel-good factor will be enough to sustain us as the memories fade into the distance. They offered a brilliant vision of teamwork, volunteerism and a global community united, but it will take a much deeper change in society to turn around the worrying direction in which we are going.

One man did see all this coming – a Scottish philosopher called Alasdair MacIntyre, who in 1981 published a book called *After Virtue*. It is a work of philosophy and, as such, not an easy read, but the case it makes is compelling. Ancient classical society evolved an understanding of the virtues – qualities such as courage, prudence and justice – which were necessary to create a society in which people could live whole and satisfying lives. Christianity built on this foundation and added new qualities such as love, humility and forgiveness. This worldview informed and sustained European societies for the next 1500 years. Then came the 18th-century period known as the Enlightenment. Alongside the rise of modern science and many great discoveries, there was a widespread and aggressive reaction against religion, seeking to make it a matter of private faith rather than public influence. The classical virtues had been replaced by a Christian society; now the Christian society was being dismantled – or, rather, its beliefs were dismissed while its morals, or at least some of them, were kept. In reality, MacIntyre argues, the very fabric which held together society was being unravelled and, with the passing of the centuries, we have separated into a more and more distant individualism with no common values and a consequent collapse of community.

MacIntyre ends with both a striking warning and a clear way forward for those with the courage and imagination to take it. Summing up the moral disintegration which underlies the unravelling of community and society, he speaks of 'the new dark ages which are already upon us'. He adds that 'this time the barbarians are not waiting beyond the frontiers; they have already been governing us for some time'.[43] This is not, however, where the book ends, because it leads into the most extraordinary and visionary conclusion about what we need to do now.

> What matters at this stage [that is, 30 years ago] is the construction of local forms of community in which civility and the intellectual and moral life can be sustained... We are waiting not for a Godot, but for another – doubtless very different – St Benedict.

The salvation of a broken society will not come from a new monetary policy or from a new moral crusade, but from a new monasticism – and this is precisely what is emerging around the world in the first decades of the third millennium. A new but, in inspiration, profoundly old kind of church is emerging, one that, in the words of the Community of Aidan and Hilda, seeks to be in touch with the scriptures and the Spirit, the saints and the streets, the seasons and the soil. Drawing on the past but listening to the present, it draws strength from a Way of Life, a rhythm of prayer and a network of Soul Friends. Rediscovering and embracing these neglected ancient practices will produce truly adult disciples who connect deeply with God and connect God with the whole of life. In a world that increasingly seeks security in either harsh authoritarianism or rigid fundamentalism, these practices will keep us reflective, learning, listening, accountable, flexible, available, open and welcoming.

We need church leaders to envision these new ancient ways of being church and to go the distance to make them the core of our communities. We need ordinary Christians to start sharing what they are discovering and gathering clusters of community where they are. That sounds like a huge vision, and it is, but ultimately all that God needs is people like us. How do you change a nation? One person at a time. How do you create a community? When two or three gather together. We have the tools, and the time to start is now.

Appendix

To find out more about the Community of Aidan and Hilda, visit
www.aidanandhilda.org.uk. The Community can also be contacted
through its main office:

The Community of Aidan and Hilda
The Open Gate
Holy Island
Berwick-upon-Tweed
TD15 2SD

Tel: 01289 389249

To find us on Facebook, search for 'The Community of Aidan and
Hilda'.

Notes

1   Christian A. Schwarz, *Natural Church Development Handbook: A practical guide to a new approach* (British Church Growth Association, 1996).
2   Mark E. Thibodeaux, *Armchair Mystic: Easing into contemplative prayer* (St Andrew Messenger, 2001), p. 16.
3   Rick Warren, *The Purpose Driven Church* (Zondervan, 1995).
4   Ian Bradley, *The Celtic Way* (DLT, 1993). Ray Simpson, *Exploring Celtic Spirituality* (Kevin Mayhew, 2004; original edition Hodder and Stoughton, 1995). Ian Bradley is also the author of the hugely insightful *Colonies of Heaven: Celtic models for today's church* (DLT, 2000), and he has written a very healthy counterbalance to those who romanticise the period to suit their own agendas in *Celtic Christianity: Making myths and chasing dreams* (Edinburgh University Press, 1999).
5   The term 'Celtic church' is very controversial among historians, hence I introduce it in inverted commas.
6   See Ray Simpson, *A Pilgrim Way: New Celtic monasticism for everyday people* (Kevin Mayhew, 2005), pp. 55–56.
7   Andy Freeman and Pete Greig, *Punk Monk: New monasticism and the ancient art of breathing* (Kingsway, 2007), pp. 101 and 96. The inspiring and amazing story of the 24–7 movement is told in Pete Greig and Dave Roberts, *Red Moon Rising: The story of 24–7 prayer* (Kingsway, 2004).
8   Diane Kershaw, 'The Order of Mission: Being a Sent People', in Graham Cray, Ian Mobsby and Aaron Kennedy (eds), *Ancient Faith, Future Mission: New monasticism as fresh expression of church* (Canterbury Press, 2010), pp. 80–91.
9   I have fully explored Ways of Life in both the Old and New Testaments in 'Followers of the Way: Biblical Foundations for Monastic Living' in Ray Simpson, *High Street Monasteries: Fresh expressions of committed Christianity* (Kevin Mayhew, 2009), pp. 127–50.
10 Dietrich Bonhoeffer, *A Testament to Freedom: The essential writings of Dietrich Bonhoeffer* (HarperCollins, 1995), p. 424.

11 Bede, *The Ecclesiastical History of the English People* (Oxford University Press, 1999), p. 146.

12 Richard Forster, *Money, Sex and Power: The challenge to the disciplined life* (Hodder and Stoughton, 1985).

13 Harold Miller, *Finding a Personal Rule of Life* (Grove, 1987).

14 Greig and Freeman, *Punk Monk*, p. 134.

15 Bede, *Ecclesiastical History*, p. 116.

16 Bede, *Ecclesiastical History*, pp. 212, 213.

17 In the Community of Aidan and Hilda we are currently working on how we ensure that the Community welcomes lesbian, gay, bisexual and transgender people who seek to follow Christ wholeheartedly, following our Way of Life. We acknowledge that some of them sincerely and in good conscience believe that committed, faithful, lifelong same-sex relationships are not contrary to the teaching of scripture, and that the relevant passages may be differently interpreted.

18 To learn about his process in detail, visit www.fows.org and search for 'The Baxter Model' (exact phrase).

19 Bede, 'Life of Cuthbert', in *The Age of Bede*, J.F. Webb (trans.), D.H. Farmer (ed.) (Penguin, 1965), p. 71.

20 Columba Stewart OSB, *The World of the Desert Fathers* (SLG Press, 1986), pp. 1–2, emphasis added.

21 Benedicta Ward SLG, *The Wisdom of the Desert Fathers* (SLG Press, 1975), p. 23.

22 Ward, *Wisdom of the Desert Fathers*, p. 7.

23 Stewart, *World of the Desert Fathers*, p. 22.

24 Ray Simpson, *A Guide for Soul Friends: The art of the spiritual companion* (Kevin Mayhew, 2008), p. 8.

25 This version of the Examen can be found on the website: www.ignatianspirituality.com.

26 Josephus, *The Antiquities of the Jews*, 4.212.

27 Cheslyn Jones, Geoffrey Wainwright, Edward Yarnold SJ, Paul Bradshaw (eds), *The Study of Liturgy*, revised edition (SPCK, 1992), p. 400.

28 Anglicans go to www.churchofengland.org/prayer-worship.aspx; Roman Catholics try www.universalis.com. I am not certain which site to recommend for Orthodox church members but if you do a search you will probably know better than me what to look for!

29 Ray Simpson, *Prayer Rhythms for Busy People*, first published by Kevin Mayhew in 2005.

30   Greig and Roberts, *Red Moon Rising*. See also *Punk Monk* for more on how the movement has developed further.

31   For those of you still struggling to get to grips with current technology, Twitter is a way of sending short messages to groups of people. Along with other forms of social media it has proved an amazingly useful means of serious as well as casual communication.

32   See, for example, Phil Potter, *The Challenge of Cell Church* (BRF, 2001).

33   See Bradley, *Colonies of Heaven*, and Ray Simpson, *Church of the Isles: A prophetic strategy for renewal* (Kevin Mayhew, 2003).

34   Ray Simpson, *Soul Friendship: Celtic insights into spiritual mentoring* (Hodder and Stoughton, 1999), pp. 179–188.

35   Uinseann Ó Maidín OCR, *The Celtic Monk: Rules and writings of the early Irish monks* (Cistercian Publications, 1996), p. 122.

36   John C. Maxwell, *Developing the Leader Within You* (Thomas Nelson, 2012), p. viii.

37   John C. Maxwell, *Thinking For A Change* (Warner Business, 1993).

38   Ray Simpson, *Waymarks for the Journey: Daily prayer to change your world* (Kevin Mayhew Ltd, 2009).

39   Simpson, *Guide For Soul Friends*.

40   Sue Pickering, *Spiritual Direction: A practical introduction* (Canterbury Press, 2008).

41   Gordon Jeff, *Spiritual Direction for Every Christian* (SPCK, 2nd edition, 2007).

42   Interestingly, having retired, he is now involved in the early stages of creating a new Christian community with others in another part of the country. Clearly God was at work, but not in the way we first thought!

43   Alasdair MacIntyre, *After Virtue: A study in moral theory* (Gerald Duckworth, 1981), p. 263.

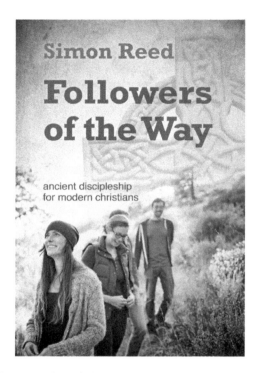

If, in simple terms, discipleship is about connecting more deeply with God and connecting God with the whole of life, Simon Reed argues, we're looking at a lifelong process for which we require long-term skills rather than short-term courses. The Celtic and Desert Christians, drawing on Old and New Testament practices, taught and modelled how to do this through the practice of living by a Way of Life. By drawing together today's need for disciples and Celtic Christianity, *Followers of the Way* inspires authentic Christian discipleship for the contemporary world.

Followers of the Way
Ancient discipleship for modern Christians
Simon Reed
978 0 85746 538 2 £7.99

brfonline.org.uk

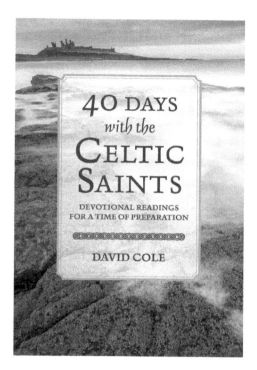

The life stories of the Celtic saints are inspirational. They demonstrate great and unassuming faith, often in the face of insurmountable difficulties. In *40 Days with the Celtic Saints*, David Cole draws us to relate our own life journey and developing relationship with God into the life story of the Celtic saint of the day. A corresponding biblical text and blessing encourages and motivates us to transform our lives for today's world in the light of such historic faith.

40 Days with the Celtic Saints
Devotional readings for a time of preparation
David Cole
978 0 85746 548 1 £7.99

brfonline.org.uk

BRF

Transforming
lives and communities

Christian growth and understanding of the Bible

Resourcing individuals, groups and leaders in churches for their own spiritual journey and for their ministry

Church outreach in the local community

Offering two programmes that churches are embracing to great effect as they seek to engage with their local communities and transform lives

Teaching Christianity in primary schools

Working with children and teachers to explore Christianity creatively and confidently

Children's and family ministry

Working with churches and families to explore Christianity creatively and bring the Bible alive

parenting for faith

Visit **brf.org.uk** for more information on BRF's work

brf.org.uk

The Bible Reading Fellowship (BRF) is a Registered Charity (No. 233280)